Ferdinand Toennies

ON SOCIOLOGY: PURE, APPLIED, AND EMPIRICAL

THE HERITAGE OF SOCIOLOGY

A Series Edited by Morris Janowitz

Ferdinand Toennies

ON SOCIOLOGY: PURE, APPLIED, AND EMPIRICAL

Selected Writings

Edited and with an Introduction by

WERNER J. CAHNMAN AND
RUDOLF HEBERLE

THE UNIVERSITY OF CHICAGO PRESS

CHICAGO AND LONDON

ISBN: 0–226–80607–3 (clothbound)
0–226–80608–1 (paperbound)
Library of Congress Catalog Card Number: 70–127822

THE UNIVERSITY OF CHICAGO PRESS, CHICAGO 60637
The University of Chicago Press, Ltd., London

Contents

III.　PURE SOCIOLOGY

IV.　EMPIRICAL SOCIOLOGY

V.　APPLIED SOCIOLOGY

Introduction

I

THE PRESENT VOLUME on Toennies differs from other volumes in the *Heritage of Sociology* series. The wide range of Toennies' work and the sheer extension of it, in combination with the difficulties of interpretation and the fact that very little thus far has been available to English-speaking readers, made it advisable to devote two volumes of this series to Ferdinand Toennies. The first volume assumes the pattern of a "Reader," presenting selections from Toennies' sociological writings with brief connecting texts. A second volume will contain papers on various aspects of Toennies' work along with a documentation of the relation of his work to those of Marx, Spencer, Durkheim and Weber.

In addition, the first volume differs from other volumes in the series because it represents more than what is still alive of a classic author's work. While Durkheim's, Simmel's, and Max Weber's writings are largely known to American social scientists through translations, such is not the case with Toennies, Charles P. Loomis' meritorious translation of *Gemeinschaft und Gesellschaft* (1940) notwithstanding. To be sure, Toennies was well known to the founding fathers of American sociology—we will return to this point later—but they read German fluently and needed no translations. However, the close contact with German literary and scientific developments which they had maintained was fatally weakened in the wake of World War I. Consequently, when Toennies collected some of the most important of the numerous papers, articles, and reviews which he had published previously in scholarly journals in the remarkable volumes of *Soziologische Studien und Kritiken* (1924, 1926, 1929) and in *Fortschritt und Soziale Entwicklung* (1926) and when he finally completed his *Einfuehrung in die Soziologie* (1931), these publications failed to make an impact. Soon afterward, the Hitler catastrophe engulfed Toennies' entire work. It follows that the pieces which we have translated come to American social scientists as a substantially new thing, and are likely to mark the emergence of Toennies as a major contributor to the heritage of sociology.

It is only seemingly contradictory to what has been just stated that *Gemeinschaft und Gesellschaft*, even without the clarification which Toennies provided in his later writings, has become one of the most influential books in modern sociology. Out of these two title words, along with Durkheim's "solidarity" and "anomie" and Weber's "bureaucracy" and "charismatic authority," one could construct the edifice of sociological conceptualization, even if all the other pieces were lost. But, as Hans Freyer has observed, the influence which Toennies' slim volume has exerted all around the globe, the German-speaking countries included, has remained "anonymous and almost subterranean" in character: everybody talks about *Gemeinschaft und Gesellschaft*, but hardly anybody has read the book from cover to cover, and those who have read it have, more often than not, largely misunderstood its message. The most frequent misunderstanding is the one of "misplaced concreteness." The sociostructural terms *Gemeinschaft* and *Gesellschaft*, along with their social-psychological counterparts "essential will" and "arbitrary will," have been taken as classifications of factual realities when, indeed, they are meant to be comprehended—thought of, as it were—as "normal" concepts or "ideal-typical" constructs; not as concretely distinguishable categories but as intellectually distillable elements of a society (a *"Scheidung,"* not an *"Unterscheidung,"* to use Toennies' own words). To quote oneself (from W. J. Cahnman and A. Boskoff, *Sociology and History*, p. 110), one can say that "thus, a 'family,' 'clan,' 'village,' 'friendship' may serve as approximate examples of *'Gemeinschaft,'* but they are *'Gemeinschaft'* only to the extent to which they coincide with the ideal conceptual image of *'Gemeinschaft.'* 'City,' 'state,' 'industry,' 'public opinion' may serve as examples of '*Gesellschaft*' in the same way. In other words, viewed in the light of normal concepts, actual societies, especially of the '*Gesellschaft*' type, are always mixed." Similarly, "essential will" and "arbitary will" are pure types of volition; they are aspects of a total psychic reality, not mutually exclusive concrete parts of it.

In Germany of late, the misunderstanding has been carried even farther. In the 1920s, but especially after 1945, in the light of the Hitlerian *Goetterdaemmerung*, Toennies was thought of being a romantic, in the sense of posing as a *laudator temporis acti* when he was actually a disciple, in part, of romantic philosophy in his emphasis on will and emotion as a substratum of, but not a substitute for, the rationality which is inherent in the human condition. He was accused of idealizing *Gemeinschaft* when he merely stressed its raw pristinity and unreflected innocence as against the deliberate calculation of advantage and disadvantage and the weighing of ends against means in *Gesellschaft*. He was pilloried as the seducer of youth because *Gemeinschaft* became the catchword of the exuberant protest of the youth movement against the false pretensions and the mechanized life style of bourgeois society; he was even made responsible for unwittingly blunting the edge of opposition against the abuse by the Nazi demagogues of such a conglomerate term as *Volksgemeinschaft*; by the same token, Toennies could have been made a "precursor"—a favorite term of *post factum* semiwisdom—of National Socialism because he saw in socialism (of a very different kind, to be sure) a hope for the future. I refrain from mentioning names at this point, except for the one of Ralf Dahrendorf. What he has to say about Toennies (in *Gesellschaft und Demokratie in Deutschland*, pp. 151 ff.) deserves reference because it is so typical of the misinterpretation of Toennies as an enemy of "modernity" as to be almost a caricature of it. Dahrendorf, in his interpretation, does precisely what Toennies, in his writings, does not, namely, to confront "a beautiful *Gemeinschaft* of emotions in the past" with "a heartless contractual *Gesellschaft* in the present"; after thus confounding concept and reality, he concludes that the bogeyman whom he has put up never existed and that *Gemeinschaft*, if it ever existed, wasn't as "agreeable" as he thinks Toennies had made it out to be, because it contained "illness and early death, hunger and war, dependence and humiliation" along with a presumed "harmony" of feelings.

No doubt, these evils, like many others, are ever present, and they are disturbing wherever they are found, but they are not, as Dahrendorf erroneously assumes, "the outcome of human essential will"—they are the negation of it. Dahrendorf further assumes erroneously, as far as the interpretation of Toennies is concerned, that an "authoritarian political order" is identical with *Gemeinschaft*, and he then assures his readers that this Don Quichotesque windmill is not "rational" when Toennies, in fact, discerns both authoritarianism and fellowship in *Gemeinschaft* as well as in *Gesellschaft*, but ascribes increasing rationality to the processes of *Gesellschaft*. Dahrendorf caps the confusion when he alleges that Toennies' intention is "to devalue contract and conflict, law and human autonomy." In Toennies' view, the positive value of *Gesellschaft* consists in pitting law and contract against the element of conflict that is inherent in human autonomy. Dahrendorf inadvertently is correct when he finds *Gesellschaft*, historically speaking, nearly identical with "modernity," but incorrect when he thinks that this is a statement *contra* Toennies. Toennies sees the shadows in the development of modern society which—surely—we all ought to be aware of, but also its inexorable necessity. As the reader of this volume will soon come to know, Toennies affirms the value of rationality as the mark of maturity and the essence of the scientific spirit. Psychoanalytically speaking, the recently fashionable German disparagement of Toennies, of which Dahrendorf is a pronounced example, may be recognizable as a displacement of guilt feelings, but that does not decide the issue. However, Toennies' comment from the first preface of *Gemeinschaft und Gesellschaft* (1887) would seem to be justified: "I shall not be responsible both for erroneous explications and for presumably clever applications. People who are not trained in conceptual thinking better abstain from passing judgment."

It must be admitted, though, that Toennies does not make it easy to fully comprehend his famous treatise. This has much to do with his style of writing, but also with the nature of his conceptualization. Toennies does not write in the approved scientific fashion, starting with hypothesis, proceeding to proof, and ending with conclusion. Rather, he presents his case after the manner of a musical composition, with two doubly intoned *leitmotivs* (essential will—*Gemeinschaft;* and arbitrary will—*Gesellschaft*) and intricately intertwined variations on the fourfold theme. In addition, he intertwines conceptual analysis with factual explication in such a way that the reader cannot always be sure whether the author refers to a "normal concept" or to a historical trend. It would be adequate to say that Toennies presents a theory of sociation that is universally valid, but that he uses this theory to illuminate the course of modern history. As a result of the multiple composition of Toennies' thinking, his style of writing is full of assumptions, allusions, and polemical asides. But the nature of his conceptualization and the thrust of his argument are clear if one considers the totality of his work in addition to the youthful work of genius that is *Gemeinschaft und Gesellschaft.*

Toennies divides the total field of sociology into general and special sociology. By general sociology, he refers to areas of inquiry that are sociologically relevant without, in his view, belonging to sociology proper, such as social biology (chiefly, physical anthropology), demography, and social psychology. These subfields, which are now securely included within sociology or anthropology, are of no more than passing interest to Toennies. His enduring interest belongs exclusively to what he calls special sociology. He subdivides special sociology into pure, applied, and empirical sociology. Pure sociology, frequently characterized as theoretical sociology, is more precisely designated as philosophical sociology: it deals with pure concepts, static norms, basic ideas, and their interrelationships. These concepts, norms, and ideas refer to human volition, and are requisites for the understanding of social structure. Applied sociology, which is likewise theoretical in nature, applies the static concepts of pure sociology to the dynamic processes of history. It has been labeled a philosophy of history, but is actually a sociology of history or, in contemporary parlance, a theory of social change. Empirical sociology, or sociography, aims at the accurate description and analysis of human relations. It uses chiefly quantitative methods, but also interviews and other tools of detailed investigation. Whenever possible, it strives for mathematical clarity of relationships. It follows that pure and applied sociology, while conceptually distinct, are not easily kept apart in analysis: pure ideas must be illustrated by reference to historical reality, and social processes must be understood in the light of pure ideas. But the relation of empirical research to pure theory is more complex.

In order to understand the nature of this connection, one must be aware of the multiple points of departure in Toennies' thinking. He starts from a natural law conception of man and the state which had been most radically formulated by Thomas Hobbes, and also by Spinoza, and which is most virulently expressed in the writings of the classical economists, and he finds there the model of *Gesellschaft;* but he complements the rational procedure of natural law with the empiricist and experientalist approach of the historical schools of law and economics, of romantic philosophy and the theory of evolution, and he derives from them, as well as from older sources, the model of *Gemeinschaft.* Man by nature is a social being in *Gemeinschaft* and an initially asocial being in *Gesellschaft;* but *Gesellschaft* makes for social relations through convention and law. In his paper on "The Nature of Sociology," Toennies says that both theses, that man is a social being, and that he is an asocial being, are correct and that they complement each other; yet, in his paper "A Prelude to Sociology," he adds that it would be inaccurate to say that the organic (historical) and the mechanical (rationalistic) view are both "right" and that they are to be combined in a synthesis; the organic view, he means to say, precedes the rationalistic view logically and historically; *Gesellschaft* is derived from *Gemeinschaft* in the same sense in which arbitrary will is derived from essential will, reflection from emotion. Yet it must be remembered that all of these are not categories but elements, and that they are "things of thought"; in the life that is lived, they are never found pure and alone. It must further be understood that essential will is not identical with drive or instinct. Volition always involves thought; but it makes a difference whether thought is in the service of vital processes or whether thought gains independence, as it were, and pursues its own ends.

The latter point is of decisive importance for the understanding of the sociology of Toennies. Many deliberations, of which we can indicate only a few, must be anchored here. One can see a number of reasons, apart from those mentioned above, why Toennies' sociology was widely misunderstood. What he had to say appealed to neither party in the *Methodenstreit:* he emphasized the primacy of life over thought, yet he delineated the victorious progress of rationality which he considered to be a psychological and historical necessity. With Hobbes and Spinoza, he held that scientific inquiry proceeds from cause to effect; but, with Schopenhauer, he believed that as the external world is moved by causality, so the internal world is moved by will, and that social processes must be understood from the inside out, that is, as conditioned by the varieties of human volition and their contradictory indications. This makes Toennies a dialectician and a phenomenologist and brings him near to the organic view of the symbolic interactionists, who reached similar conclusions from different points of departure. Toennies would have endorsed Cooley's sentence, "The imaginations which people have of one another are the solid facts of society." But he would have added that imagination must be seen as turning into action through the agency of the human will. We will have to say more about these linkages of thought in the second volume.

The present volume should do away with the notion that Toennies thought of *Gemeinschaft* as "good" and *Gesellschaft* as "bad"; his repudiation of value judgments in scholarship is as pronounced as Max Weber's, and it is documented already in the preface to the first edition of *Gemeinschaft und Gesellschaft;* it has been repeated on later occasions. The present volume also ought to do away with the related notion that Toennies assumes a world without conflict. Rather, what he means to say is that social relations, as envisaged in pure sociology, are positive, affirmative relations, either of the *Gemeinschaft* or the *Gesellschaft* type, or at least predominantly of one or the other type. Negative, or hostile, relations are acknowledged, but they are designated as being asocial, or even antisocial, in character; in a pure *Gemeinschaft*, they are nonexistent *ex definitione;* in a pure *Gesellschaft,* they are neutralized by the legitimately exercised power of the state. Hostile relations, such as crime, delinquency, marital discord, strikes, lockouts, riots, wars, and, even more so, the radical negation of social bonds that occurs in suicide, are therefore pathological. To use medical analogy, *Gemeinschaft* and *Gesellschaft* as well as their psychic correlates essential will and arbitrary will, like health, are normal concepts or "things of thought"; they must be assumed. But manifestations of pathology, hostility, illness, and death are actual occurrences; they must be researched. They are deviations from basic assumptions; they are social problems. A statement of this kind marks the place of empirical sociology in Toennies' scheme of special sociology. Toennies himself used the term pathology in his paper "Sozialwissenschaftliche Forschungsinstitute" (*Forschungsinstitute—Ihre Geschichte, Organisation und Ziele,* Hamburg 1930) and elsewhere; one is therefore justified in saying that Toennies' published work as a whole uses not so much a dichotomy of *Gemeinschaft* and *Gesellschaft* as a trichotomy of *Gemeinschaft, Gesellschaft,* and pathology. There are pathologies of *Gemeinschaft* and pathologies of *Gesellschaft.* Clearly, these are not found in pure sociology, but they intrude into applied sociology, and they constitute the dominant theme in empirical sociology. Methodologically, pure sociology, dealing in essences, uses a phenomenological approach; applied sociology, analyzing processes, a dialectical approach; and empirical sociology, investigating social problems, a positivistic approach. If this is understood, the three sociologies of Toennies, although they speak in different tongues, will be seen as closely interrelated and as a unit in thought.

II

Ferdinand Toennies (26 July 1855–9 April 1936) was born on the parental farm in the county of Eiderstedt in Schleswig-Holstein, Germany; he spent his childhood there and, after his father's retirement, in the nearby town of Husum, always within sight and sound of the North Sea. His mother's family—her maiden name was Mau—hailed from East Holstein, and was predominantly a family of Protestant ministers and of scholars. His father's family was of Frisian origin. The Frisian people, who inhabit the northern provinces of the Netherlands as well as a coastal rim in Germany stretching from the Dutch to the Danish border, have maintained themselves as an independent peasantry, free from feudal domination, from the early Middle Ages until modern times. It would not be correct, however, to think of Toennies as being of peasant origin in anything like the accepted meaning of the term. His father grazed meat cattle that were shipped to markets in Hamburg and in England; in addition, he had an interest in a provincial bank. But it is correct that Toennies throughout his life remained emotionally tied to "the gray town by the sea," as Husum was called by the poet Storm, whom Toennies knew and adored, and generally to land and folk in Schleswig-Holstein. Although a scholar's scholar, he had an easy way with the common people, a trait that made him a perfect interviewer.

His father's means enabled Toennies to study philosophy, history, classic languages, and archaeology, and, later, economics and statistics at the universities of Jena, Bonn, Leipzig, Berlin, and Tuebingen; at the latter university, he received a doctorate of philosophy in the field of classical philology in 1877. In 1881 he became a *Privatdozent* at the University of Kiel (in philosophy) on the strength of a first draft of what was six years later to become his famous book *Gemeinschaft und Gesellschaft*. He lived in Kiel and Hamburg and later in Eutin, a small town between Kiel and Luebeck, but did little teaching, partly because he did not enjoy the formal obligations connected with teaching, partly because his independence of mind, his socialist leanings, his support of working class movements, and—apparently—his membership in the Ethical Culture Society made him persona non grata with the powerful chief of personnel of the central university administration in Prussia. He became a full professor (appointed to a chair of economics) only in 1913, but applied for emeritus status already in 1916; however, as emeritus, he resumed teaching, this time in sociology, from 1921 to 1933, when he was summarily dismissed by the National Socialist regime. His erratic career notwithstanding, Toennies enjoyed a high reputation as a scholar.

From 1909 to 1933 he was a member of and president of the *Deutsche Gesellschaft fuer Soziologie,* which he founded together with Georg Simmel, Werner Sombart, Max Weber, Rudolf Goldscheid, and others. He was a co-founder and first president of the *Societas Hobbesiana* (Toennies was a Hobbes scholar of the first order), a member of the *Verein fuer Sozialpolitik,* the *Gesellschaft fuer Soziale Reform,* the *Institut International de Sociologie,* the English and Japanese sociological societies, and a honorary member of the American Sociological Society, among others. Toennies attended many international scholarly congresses, but he was especially at home in England. From his youth, when he searched British archives for Hobbes manuscripts, to his old age, he remained an admirer and disciple of English scholarship; as far as the social sciences are concerned, he repeatedly testified to his indebtedness especially to Herbert Spencer and Henry Sumner Maine.

Toennies was not a liberal in the sense of the Manchester liberalism of the nineteenth century; nor was he a supporter of the sham splendor and vainglory of the Hohenzollern empire. He was a democrat, a republican, a freethinker, a socialist of a kind, and a devoted supporter of the labor movement; he was intensely interested in trade unions, consumer cooperatives, and adult education, especially workers' education. One can say that he was conservative in temperament but radical in conviction. Although he believed that a scholar should not be a member of a political party, he eventually joined the Social Democratic party in 1932, in view of the rising threat of the Nazi movement. He wanted to stand up and be counted. We will publish examples of his anti-Nazi articles from this period in the second volume.

Toennies' contacts with, and his influence upon, American sociology constitute a fascinating topic which can be referred to at this point only in a cursory manner. Toennies was most appreciative of Lewis H. Morgan's *Ancient Society,* which he called "a standard work of sociology"; he was especially impressed by its congruence with the basic tenets of Marxism. Marx and Engels, as well as Morgan, emphasize the importance of human relations at work and of technology; and so does Toennies. Among the fifty-

five non-German authors (along with thirty-six from Germany
and Austria) whose work Toennies reviews in Volume III of *Soziologische Studien und Kritiken* are nine American authors; the
most important names, apart from Morgan, are Small, Ward, Gid-
dings, Walter Lippman, and Mark Baldwin. Toennies' contacts
with Albion W. Small seem to have been especially close. He was
invited to participate in the Congress of Arts and Science of the
Universal Exposition in St. Louis, Missouri, in 1904, apparently
at the initiative of the exposition's vice-presidents, Albion W.
Small, the founder of the department of sociology at the University
of Chicago, and Hugo Muensterberg, the German-American psychologist at Harvard University. Among the American social scientists whom Toennies met at St. Louis were Charles A. Ellwood,
William I. Thomas, and Edward A. Ross. The paper which he read
at St. Louis, "The Present Problems of Social Structure," was
published in *The American Journal of Sociology* in 1905, and is
reproduced in this volume. Toennies was among the early editors
of that journal.

Toennies' work was well known to Robert E. Park. Toennies is
quoted three times in Park's and Burgess' influential *Introduction
to Sociology*, and Park's dichotomy of "family" versus "market-
place" clearly is an adaptation from Toennies, turning what had
been an ideal type into a real type—a very Parkian procedure.
Park himself acknowledges (in *The Problem of Cultural Differences*, 1931) that the dichotomy of "sacred" versus "secular" societies is directly derived from Toennies' concepts of *Gemeinschaft*
and *Gesellschaft*. Two of Park's foremost students, Howard Becker
and Robert Redfield, later have elaborated on this dichotomy and
on the related dichotomy of "folk" versus "city." Generally, however, Toennies' influence had turned subterranean: he was quoted
and even utilized without quotation, but not read. The familiar
misinterpretation of Toennies' basic theorems, that they idealized
the country and pilloried the city, appealed to many American
sociologists in the 1920's. To those who actually read and—at least
in part—understood Toennies belongs Louis Wirth, whose paper
on "The Sociology of Ferdinand Toennies" appeared in the
AJS in 1927. Surely, Louis Wirth's paper on "Urbanism as a Way

of Life" (1938) is inspired by a Toenniesian conceptualization. By way of contrast, Robert M. McIver's references to Toennies in his books on *Community* (1929) and *Society* (1937) seem to be far off the mark. Pitirim A. Sorokin's treatment in *Contemporary Sociological Theories* (1928) is more perceptive, although it is marred by Sorokin's mannerism of finding everything a later author says "adumbrated" in earlier authors. Albert Salomon's brilliant obituary of Toennies in *Social Research* (1936) went largely unnoticed, and so did Karl J. Arndt's and C. L. Folse's translation of Toennies' article "The Concept of Law and Human Progress" in *Social Forces* (1940). An effective breakthrough came with Talcott Parsons' "Note on Gemeinschaft and Gesellschaft" in *The Structure of Social Action* (1937). Both Albert Salomon's article and Parsons' "Note" (the latter with a notable addition acknowledging that the "pattern variables" are derived from Toennies' basic concepts) will be reproduced in the second volume. We refrain here from referring specifically to Rudolf Heberle's various papers and articles on Toennies. With Charles P. Loomis' translation of *Gemeinschaft und Gesellschaft* under the title *Fundamental Concepts of Sociology* (1940), we enter into a new phase. Its effects were delayed, however, by World War II and its aftermath; they become manifest only now.

III

Else Brenke's bibliography ("Schriften von Ferdinand Toennies aus den Jahren 1875–1935" in: *Reine und Angewandte Soziologie—Eine Festgabe fuer Ferdinand Toennies zu seinem 80. Geburtstage* (Leipzig: Hans Buske, 1936), although not entirely complete, contains over six hundred items, the harvest of a lifetime. To be sure, many of these items are popularizations of scholarly papers, some are repetitious. But even if half of the six hundred publications are laid aside, there remains a stupendous output of scholarly productivity to choose from. In order to decide on the selections that were to go into the present volume, the first consideration was to exclude those publications that were already easily accessible in English, especially *Gemeinschaft und Gesell-schaft* (ed. Chas. P. Loomis, now available, under the title *Com-*

munity and Society, as a Harper Torchbooks paperback), *Custom* trans. F. A. Borenstein, 1961) and the paper translated by Arndt and Folse in *Social Forces* (1940). However, we included the St. Louis Exposition paper of 1904, because it could hardly be considered easily accessible, and two brief passages from *Gemeinschaft und Gesellschaft* (using Loomis' translation, but modifying it in part), because they are indispensable for the argument which our selections intend to present, yet likely to be overlooked by the casual reader of the Harper Torchbook edition. We then gathered the selections into four major parts. Part I deals with the formation of Toennies' "pure" concepts, meaning normal concepts and ideal-typical constructs, especially the basic types of *Gemeinschaft* and *Gesellschaft*. Particular attention is given to the emergence of the ideal type concept from Toennies' interpretation of the philosophy of Thomas Hobbes. Part II deals with the elaboration of these concepts in papers which Toennies published in the years 1899–1924. It is very difficult, if not impossible, to grasp what Toennies meant to say in his classic book of 1887 without an intimate knowledge of these four explanatory papers. Part III, then, presents Toennies' mature treatment of pure sociology in selected chapters from *Einfuehrung in die Soziologie*. What had been presented rather poetically in *Gemeinschaft und Gesellschaft* is here scientifically clarified and at the same time elaborated. Part IV deals with empirical sociology, but in an unsatisfactory and sketchy way owing to the fact that almost all of Toennies' numerous papers on topics of empirical sociology are very long, full of tabulations, and hardly excerptible. However, to make good for the omission, a paper reviewing Toennies' total output in empirical sociology (or sociography) will be offered in the second volume. Part V deals with applied sociology, that is, chiefly with the theory of social change and the theory of public opinion; public opinion must be understood both as an element of social change and as a result of it. Toennies' theory of social change, which was never systematically elaborated by Toennies himself, likewise will be treated in the second volume.

A few things must be said about the principles which guided the translation. To translate Toennies requires a great deal of sensitivity. He assumes that the reader has a considerable knowl-

edge of the philosophical, sociological, and historiographical literature in the major European languages, and he writes a very
personal and rather discursive style. In addition, description and
analysis, assertion and polemics are often intermingled. Without
a subtle sympathetic insight, one can easily read out of a Toenniesian sentence a meaning that the author never intended to put
in. At times, one passage is understandable only if one remembers
another passage that is complementary to it. Consequently, all
translations had to be checked and rechecked repeatedly, occasionally almost to the point of a retranslation. The terminology had
to be brought in agreement with current sociological usage. Passages that were too brief had to be expanded somewhat while
others that seemed to be verbose had to be curtailed—all this without violating the basic requirement of faithfulness to the author's
intentions. We can assure the reader only that we have tried to
do our best, not that we have entirely succeeded.

Toennies' terminology is another matter. As a rule, we have
not translated the key words *Gemeinschaft* and *Gesellschaft* although occasionally we have said "community" and "association."
Wherever we said "communal" and "associational," we have put
the words *Gemeinschaft*-like and *Gesellschaft*-like in brackets. By
"community," the reader must not understand a territorial or administrative entity, but what is held in common, what makes for
cohesion, what provides bond among men. Occasionally, the meaning of the word "community" comes near to the one of "communion," as in intimate friendship and similar relations that are
beyond question. Of course, initially the local community, the
community of blood and the community of minds and hearts were
one and the same thing, but this unity has been lost. Only fragments of community exist in our life, making for widespread un-
easiness and a sense of alienation. We have translated *Gesellschaft*
as "association" rather than as "society," because in the word "association" the meaning of choice and purpose comes clearly to the
fore while "society" is generally understood as referring to an
overall entity; and we ought not call the part by the same name
as we do the whole. It is, however, interesting to note that not so
long ago (for instance, with Hegel), "civic society" referred to
the economic nexus as against either the intimate "family-society"

or the supreme power of the state. Now the market aspect of human relations is all-pervasive.

The psychic correlates of *Gemeinschaft* and *Gesellschaft*, *Wesenwille* and *Kuerwille*, are rendered as "essential will" and "arbitrary will." This differs from Loomis' usage of "natural will" and "rational will" because this usage might be conducive to something like Wundt's mistaken interpretation of *Wesenwille* as an instinctual drive and therefore as devoid of rationality. Rather, "essential" refers to the unity of life and thought, while "arbitrary" refers to the emergence of thought as an independent agent, with the effect that means and end may cleave apart.

Some Toenniesian terms have to be translated flexibly. For example, *Beziehung* usually is to be translated as "(social) relation" or "interaction" and *Verhaeltnis* as "relationship," but this does not hold in every instance—quite apart from the occasional usuage of *Verhaeltnis* in the very concrete sense of "affair" or "liaison." By and large, *Verbindung* ("union") is based on essential will, and *Verein* ("association") on arbitrary will, while *Verband* refers to any "organized group"; yet, *Verbindung* and *Verband* at times are used interchangeably. *Gebilde* and *Bezugsgebilde* are frequently, but not always, to be translated as "social structures" or "institutions." Still more complex is the case of *Herrschaft* and *Genossenschaft*. *Herrschaft* is translated as "dominion," "domination," "authority," "control," depending on the context, but *Genossenschaft* can either be rendered as "fellowship" or, in the case of a *Konsumgenossenschaft*, as "cooperative"; the adjective *genossenschaftlich* may be translated either as "cooperative" or as "egalitarian." It must further be understood that *Genossenschaft* is typically *Gemeinschaft*-like, while *Herrschaft* can occur either in *Gemeinschaft* or in *Gesellschaft*. Frequently, in order not to mislead the reader, we have put the German term in brackets beside whatever English translation was preferred in a particular instance.

The translations are by Carola Toennies Atkinson, A. B. Ashton, Werner J. Cahnman, Ursula Fritzsche, Rudolf Heberle, E. G. Jacoby, and Kaethe Mengelberg. Carola Atkinson, with the assistance of Rudolf Heberle, translated the chapters from the *Introduc-*

tion to Sociology; A. B. Ashton translated *Progress and Social Development;* Werner J. Cahnman *My Relation to Sociology,* the first preface to *Gemeinschaft und Gesellschaft, Power and Value of Public Opinion, The Concept of Gemeinschaft, Prelude to Sociology,* and, together with Kaethe Mengelberg, the second preface to *Gemeinschaft und Gesellschaft* and *The Divisions of Sociology;* Ursula Fritzsche, together with Cahnman, *Historicism, Rationalism, and the Industrial System;* Rudolf Heberle, the chapters dealing with empirical sociology; and E. G. Jacoby, the selections from Hobbes, *The Nature of Sociology,* and the concluding piece from *The Spirit of the Modern Age.* However, all translations were checked by Cahnman and rechecked by Heberle, to ensure the necessary unity of style and interpretation. The editors assume full responsibility for whatever miscarriages may have occurred.

The editors worked together in perfect harmony; both selections and translations are our common responsibility. Parts I and II of this Introduction were written by Cahnman but approved by Heberle; Part III as well as the linkage text are a cooperative product. It must be revealed, moreover, that there were two assistant editors without whose help the arduous work that is now behind us could not have been completed: Franziska Toennies Heberle and E. G. Jacoby. Franziska Heberle provided the personal touch in our ongoing conversation as well as the index; E. G. Jacoby (of New Zealand), apart from his participation in the business of translation, fashioned the selected bibliography and kept up a continuous correspondence with the editors. Jacoby not only is a student of Toennies; his knowledge of every nook and cranny of Toenniesiana is so superb that it would have been plainly impossible to proceed without him. Gisella L. Cahnman, fortunately an exceedingly busy person herself, had to endure her husband's unavailability most of the time. Cahnman's students at Rutgers University tolerated frequent references to Toennies in the theory and social change classes. Morris Janowitz was a patient and generous general editor. Also, the financial assistance of the Rutgers Research Council is gratefully acknowledged. The most important person in the entire enterprise, the prospective reader, cannot be characterized. It is hoped, however, that he will be satisfied.

I. Formation of Concepts

EDITORS' NOTE. *The chapters combined in Part I under the heading* Formation of Concepts *are decisive for the understanding of Toennies' sociology. Most of them were written early in life; but we are fortunate, indeed, to have from Toennies' pen an autobiographical piece, written late in life, "when the shadows of the evening are falling"; this is an acknowledgment of his spiritual ancestry and a clear statement of his mature scholarly convictions.*

The first and the second prefaces to the significant work of his youth, Gemeinschaft und Gesellschaft, *written in 1887 and 1912, respectively, are likewise indispensable if one wishes to comprehend and evaluate properly the philosophic background, the scientific intention and the polemic aim of this slim but influential volume. These prefaces were not included in Charles P. Loomis' translation, and are published here in English for the first time.*

The importance of Toennies' Hobbes studies for the formation of his concepts cannot be overrated. We are referring to these studies in a special prefatory note in connection with the chapter on Normal Concepts.

1

MY RELATION TO SOCIOLOGY

I wish to characterize briefly my relation to sociology.
I had been early engaged in philosophical studies, and approx-
imately since 1877 these were centered on Thomas Hobbes, especially on his writings about the philosophy of law and government.
From this point of departure the path led generally into the English
literature about these matters, and within a short time this showed
me the way to Herbert Spencer. From Spencer I turned back to
Auguste Comte. Now, I had before me the two great authors in

Translated from "Mein Verhaeltnis zur Soziologie," *Soziologie von Heute:
Ein Symposium der Zeitschrift fuer Voelkerpsychologie und Soziologie,*
ed. Richard Thurnwald (Leipzig: C. L. Hirschfeld, 1932), pp. 103–22.
Considerably abridged, especially regarding the controversy with L. v.
Wiese who had critically commented on the foundations of Toennies'
sociology in *Koelner Vierteljahrshefte fuer Soziologie,* vol. 4.

L. v. Wiese had attacked Toennies on three points: first, that Toennies
thought of *Gemeinschaft* as "good," *Gesellschaft* as "bad," which constituted an impermissible value judgment; second, that no concrete phen-
nomenon could properly be described as either *Gemeinschaft* or *Gesellschaft;* third, that social relations could be of a negative as well as a
positive character. The gist of Toennies' reply to the first criticism is included in the selection that follows. His reply to the second criticism was
that he thought of *Gemeinschaft* and *Gesellschaft* as heuristic principles
or "normal concepts" (*Normalbegriffe*), with "ideal types" as their objects. It is fairly obvious that v. Wiese misinterpreted Toennies' position
with regard to points one and two; but the controversy with regard to the
third point cannot be resolved in a similarly clearcut manner. L. v. Wiese's
position makes good sense from a positivistic point of view while Toennies'
way of seeing things is voluntaristic in character.

sociology; Albert Schaeffle was linked to them as a German sociologist of some importance. Indeed, Schaeffle's *magnum opus*, *Bau und Leben des sozialen Koerpers*, like Spencer's work, is entirely conceived in the organicistic manner, even if it is more specific as far as the working out of the analogies is concerned. These analogies interested me very much at this time, and they made me try *pari passu* to enlarge and deepen my knowledge of biology. In the philosophy of law I received a strong impetus partly from R. v. Jhering, partly from Sir Henry Maine. In addition, I occupied myself with the specifically German literature of rational natural law, starting with Pufendorf, as well as with the historical school of law and the romantic writers, who denied the validity of natural law and supplanted it. For instance, at this time (ca. 1881), I read with vivid interest Adam Mueller's *Die Elemente der Staatskunst.*

I decided to comprehend the true meaning of natural law as well as the intentionally destructive criticism of it; consequently I reached the point where I could form for myself a picture of the entire pervasive effect of rationalism and the principle of scientific reasoning which is derived from it. As a result of all this, I attempted to understand (*verstehen*) psychologically all non-rational and somewhat less than rational modes of thought and I concluded that they could never be absolutely unreasonable (*unvernuenftig*), that they must carry their own meaning and that this meaning ultimately was reducible to human volition. I arrived at the generalization that what is social emanates from human willing, from the intention to relate to each other, a together-willing (*Zusammenwollen*), as it were; and I set myself the task of penetrating to the essence of this willing.

The study of scientific socialism contributed considerably to the clarification of my thinking. I was fervently devoted to socialism in these years: as early as 1878 I had read assiduously the first volume of Karl Marx's major work, *Das Kapital*; Rodbertus and his interpreter Adolf Wagner stimulated me for years afterward. At the same time, I was interested in ethnology. Among the works which impressed me deeply I should like to mention especially Bachofen's *Mother-Law* and an American publication, Morgan's

Ancient Society. I might have mentioned a number of other works of this kind, particularly those of English and French authors who attempted to penetrate into the supposedly earliest phases of the social life of mankind, for instance, Hearn's *The Aryan Household* and Fustel de Coulanges' *La Cité antique.* Only much later, I got acquainted with and appreciated the works of the German jurist Leist.

From these studies and thoughts derived the book *Gemeinschaft und Gesellschaft,* whose first edition bears the subtitle: *A Treatise of Communism and Socialism as Empirical Forms of Culture.* I intended to say thereby that one ought not to see in these oft-quoted slogans mere phantasies, that is, cleverly reasoned ideals and utopias, but manifestations of actual social life. Regarding communism, this was nothing new, because such concepts as original (early) communism and agrarian communism were frequently used already at that time. What I thought to elaborate, in addition, was that another concept which likewise was often mentioned as a characteristic feature of modernity, namely, "individualism," was nothing but an ideal limiting point in the grand process which leads from communism to socialism, from *Gemeinschaft* to *Gesellschaft.* In this sense, I had said already in the preface to the first edition that there is no individualism in history and culture, except as it emanates from *Gemeinschaft* and remains conditioned by it, or as it brings about and sustains *Gesellschaft.* And on the last page of the text it is said: "The whole development . . . can be conceived as a trend (tendency) from the original (simple, familylike) communism and the (rural-urban) individualism which emanates from it and is based thereon, to the independent (metropolitan-universalistic) individualism and the thereby determined (national and international) socialism." In stating it this way, I meant to say that the germs of socialism are contained already in the whole matter of formal contracts and especially in the association, so that what was involved in the parallel progress of civic society and governmental institutions (*Staat*) essentially was an enhancement of the political factor, that is, the government. In this connection, I thought both of the societal development which makes this enhancement necessary and of the "law" of the increase of governmental responsibilities of my learned protector Adolph Wagner. Always did I see in the entire historical development since the middle ages the gradual setting free of rationalism and its increasing dominance as inherently necessary processes, and especially as processes of the human mind as will. From early youth I had been led by Schopenhauer to comprehending in will the core and essence of what is human, but I never fully appreciated the metaphysical generalization and the impermissible enlargement of the concept of will which is implied in Schopenhauer's philosophy. Rather, I soon returned to the concept of will as something specifically human, as *appetitus rationalis*. For a long time I have in my thoughts tried to work out the difference within the reasonable will which would correspond to the difference between *Gemeinschaft* and *Gesellschaft*. Finally, I arrived at the following formula: "Since all mental effect, because it is human, is characterized by thinking, I am discerning will inasmuch as it contains thinking and thinking inasmuch as it contains will." I first called these concepts essential will and arbitrariness (*Wesenwille* and *Willkuer*), but replaced the latter term in the third edition by the term arbitrary will (*Kuerwille*), because of the very different and somewhat contradictory meaning which is attached to the term arbitrariness.

The theorem to which I have recently attached decisive weight for the comprehension of the entire theory has not yet been sufficiently clarified in the book, namely: that relations and associations must always be understood as autonomous, except if they are imposed from the outside. In other words, relations and associations must be understood as existing in the will of those that are related and connected by it. They are immediately present only in the consciousness (*Bewusstsein*) of the participants; this is particularly so in the case of secret societies. In the second place, to be sure, relations and associations exist also with regard to other persons and their particular relations and associations, and these other persons recognize their existence by certain characteristic features, if and when they intend to enter into a relation or association with them; this is conditioned primarily by the existence of relations and associations of a similar kind. The most important example is the recognition in international law of a state and its government by other states and their governments; these are most important events in political history. However, the same thing occurs in simpler and more private spheres, for instance, in the recognition of a union by the managers of a large-scale enterprise or the leaders of an employers' association, by which act the workers' association is recognized as actually existent and capable of entering into negotiations, precisely as in international law recognition regularly is followed by the assumption of diplomatic relations. Also, among the students at an academic institution mutual recognition of their respective associations is of similar significance.

My work in pure sociology—as I later called it—was put to rest for about two decades because theoretical problems met with very little understanding in that period. As I had been strongly interested since the days of my youth in demography and moral statistics, I devoted myself to investigations in these fields, especially in criminology. But I returned to the conceptual world of pure sociology soon after the beginning of the new century, that is, as soon as the atmosphere had become more favorable. In a paper about "The Nature of Sociology" (*Das Wesen der Soziologie*, Gehe Stiftung, 1907), I searched for a common concept for social relations (*soziale Verhaeltnisse*) and associations (*soziale Verbaende*), and for a mediating concept between them, and I thought that "social will" might be such a concept. Soon, however, I realized that "social will" is a heterogeneous concept because it doesn't refer to a concrete entity while concrete entities, in turn, come into existence only through social will. In this way I arrived at the concept of a social collective, or social collectivity (*Samtschaft*). A social collective is an enlargement of social circles, and a social circle, such as a family or a circle of friends, is to be understood as the objective unity of a multiplicity of social relations. Collectives, however, I conceive of as being of firmer texture and longer duration although, like relations and associations, they are immediately given in the thinking and willing of their members. An example is a social estate or—almost an ideal type of a collective—a political party. This makes the difference between collective and association very clear: a collective as such is unorganized, for instance, a country's nobility or, to be sure, a party; however, a collective can bring forth a formal organization, as may be observed frequently. Other examples of large-scale, unorganized collectives are a people, a society, Christendom, Protestants, Freethinkers, and others; finally mankind, at least as an idea.

After I had thus differentiated between three kinds of social entities, I might be asked why I have not combined these in the concept of the group, after the manner of other respected sociologists. I believe I have good reasons to reject the term group. The use of that term reveals unawareness of, and deviation from, the basic idea which underlies my theory of social entities, namely, that they ought to be seen and analyzed from the inside out; this does not apply to the merely external formation of groups or crowds. I observe a group of people on a street, if a dozen or more persons gather at the place of an accident or on the occasion of a brawl.[1] To be sure, it is possible to look upon phenomena of this kind sociologically; but they are not per se sociological, or social, entities. Perhaps it would have been more serviceable to use the term social configurations (*Gestalten*). I have preferred the term social entity (*Wesenheit*) for two reasons. First, I wanted to avoid the misunderstanding that the term configuration had anything to do with *Gestalt* psychology. Second, it seemed to me that the term entity pointed more decisively to the requirement of emphasizing the subjective foundation of all human associations—and this is the cardinal point of my theory.

I first developed the essential points of my entire theory in the treatise "The Divisions of Sociology" ("Einteilung der Soziologie"). With slight modification I hold on to the position taken in that treatise. It is the basis of my *Introduction to Sociology* (*Einfuehrung in die Soziologie*), which is going to appear in 1931. This *Introduction* refers almost exclusively to theoretical, or pure, sociology because pure sociology contains those concepts and theories which characterize sociology as a particular branch

[1]   Contemporary sociology does conceive of a group in psychological terms, that is, as an "inside-out" relation, while it regards a crowd as a mere aggregate.—Eds.

of scientific knowledge. However, I distinguish between pure, applied, and empirical sociology, and devote to the two latter branches a brief chapter at the end of the *Introduction*. Further, in view of the fact that scientific usage attaches a much wider meaning to the term sociology, I thought it convenient to designate this wider meaning, which includes social biology and social psychology, as general sociology, as distinguished from special sociology, which is sociology in a more specific sense. Pure sociology, then, marks the point of departure in special sociology. . . .

At this point,[2] I might say a word about the voluntaristic explication of social structures (*Gebilde*), which has been subjected to doubt by L. von Wiese. He does not want to hear anything about taking one's point of departure from the motives of men; he maintains that "nothing can be said about such generalities." I must admit that this opens up an abyss between us. The objection against my pointing to a people (*Volk*) as an example of a collective runs like this: one could find in all kinds of places numerous individuals who preferred belonging to another people, if they had the choice. I regret to have to consider this objection as invalid. The reason for the misunderstanding is that von Wiese refuses to recognize the principles which are basic for the formation of my concepts—normal concepts—and their objects—ideal types. He says that my "mode of thinking which is rooted in my native soil," namely, that a deep harmony existed between man's essential will and the conditions under which he had grown up, was nothing but an ideal, a mere fiction that was stubbornly maintained by moralists and politicians; "but it was not always in agreement with reality." I have not considered it as an "ideal," but as an ideal, or constructional, type. Consequently, it goes without saying that not all phenomena which may be named after it can actually be subsumed under it; it would seem obvious that our earth is a very particular kind of sphere and yet we use this mathematical normal concept to describe it. . . .

As far as the concepts of *Gemeinschaft* and *Gesellschaft* are concerned, it ought to be understood that I don't apply them to the

---

2   The sequence of the following sections has been reversed.—Eds.

development of a culture in such a way—as L. von Wiese seems to assume—that the former, as a period of youth, is described as "good," the latter, as a period of senescence, as "bad," with the consequence that what is good in youth is seen as derived from *Gemeinschaft* while the evil quality of senescence is derived from *Gesellschaft*. If anybody should have talked in this manner, all I can say is that he's certainly not been my pupil, for the simple reason that I consider such a way of putting it to be thoroughly erroneous. My own opinion is very different. I do not know of any condition of culture or society in which elements of *Gemeinschaft* and elements of *Gesellschaft* are not simultaneously present, that is, mixed. Moreover, although *Gemeinschaft*, too, arrives at higher and nobler forms of human relations, it is correct to say that *Gesellschaft* is the essentially variable element which enhances culture but also transforms it into civilization—to use, once again, these two concepts, which occur in this sense already in the preface to the first edition of *G. & G.*; by the way, Franz Oppenheimer emphasizes the same contradictions. The decisive factor in the emergence of *Gesellschaft*, that is, the causative factor in the tremendous revolution that culminates in *Gesellschaft*, is economic in nature, namely, trade. In my opinion, trade in its development is nothing but the capitalistic system. My evaluation of this system does not essentially differ from the one of a thousand socialists, before me, with me, and after me, and if I differ, I do so only in the sense that I am perhaps more seriously engaged in the objective analysis of the totality of the capitalistic development during the last few centuries. I do not disregard the tremendous consequences of trade, which connects places and peoples, or the achievements of trade regarding the liberation and growth of the individual forces of will and mind. Especially do I recognize that a consequence of trade is science; and with the battle of science against ignorance, superstition, and delusion I sympathize from the depth of my soul. In this respect I have never wavered: if this is not always clearly discernible in *G. & G.*, in spite of what was already on my mind at the time when it was written, then the reason for it must be sought in the limitations of this work. I have dated notes from these and still earlier years which clearly demon-

2

PREFACE TO THE FIRST EDITI

OF *GEMEINSCHAFT UND*

GESELLSCHAFT

THE CONTRAST of the historical and the rationalistic interpretations of living phenomena has in the course of the nineteenth century permeated all aspects of the sociocultural sciences. This contrast coincides essentially with the attack of empiricism and critical philosophy upon the stable system of rationalism, as it used to be represented in Germany by the Wolffian school of thought. To gain a renewed understanding of these varied approaches is therefore of no small import, if one intends, as I do, to arrive at a new analysis of the fundamental problems of social life.

It is paradoxical to say that empiricism, in spite of its decisive triumph over rationalism, at the same time is complementary to it in a formal sense. This is particularly noticeable with regard to Kant's theory of knowledge, which, claiming to reconcile the contradictions, is as much modified empiricism as it is modified rationalism. This is noticeable already with regard to Hume's pure empiricism; for Hume, too, does not inquire whether a general and necessary cognition of facts and causality actually exists; rather, he deduces conceptually the impossibility of such a cognition in much the same way in which Kant subsequently believed to be able to deduce its actuality and consequently its potentiality. Both employ a rationalistic approach, but with opposing results. Hume had presupposed empiricism with reference to perception,

---

Translated from Vorrede zur ersten Anflage (1887) of *Gemeinschaft und Gesellschaft*, according to the new edition (Darmstadt: Wissenschaftliche Buchgesellschaft, 1963), pp. xv–xxv. The last two paragraphs have been omitted.

trate how I thought and felt in my youth. Another testimony
my intensive occupation with thinkers like Hobbes and Spino
Of romantic enthusiasm, I have permitted just as much to in
ence me as I felt was objectively warranted, especially from
point of view of esthetics; in this sense I have looked upon Ad
Mueller with considerable benevolence, but, to be sure, not w
exaggerated admiration. If romanticism becomes a personal pl
losophy, it must lead the Protestant and the freethinker into t
lap of the *una sancta catholica*, because in that case he seeks em
tional tranquility and esthetic satisfaction more than truth. T
opinion that I should be capable of such a manner of thinking h
always made me smile, if not to say laugh. However, I do thin
that even in the event—which I believe would be the most favo
able regarding the present civilization—that this civilization coul
be gradually transformed into a socialistic organization of society
the end nevertheless would be inescapable. It would not be the en
of mankind, nor would it be the end of civilization or culture, bu
it would be the end of the particular civilization or culture that is
marked by the heritage of Rome.

in the sense that cognition appears as the effect of objective qualities and existential situations upon a carte blanche of the human
mind; according to Kant, perception, like thought itself, is a product of the subject's activity, even if the existentiality and coeffec-
tiveness of the objects remains granted. Following Kant, one
might say that the coincidence with respect to truth is conditioned
by the identical nature of the instruments of cognition which, beyond forms of perception and rational categories, are nothing but
idea-complexes. More specifically, the instruments of cognition
are associations of perceptions and images with names and judgments, as far as the comprehension of facts is concerned. However, if we look for the cause of given effects, we must assume definite concepts concerning the nature of *agentia* (essences, objects,
or forces) and concerning the manner in which they become effective, so that one can select necessities and certainties from a wide
range of potentialities. According to a Humean empiricism, however, such certainties cannot be reached otherwise but through
the acquired knowledge of regular temporary sequences, so that,
indeed, all associations of an equal kind are confirmed through
repetition as habits and can be interpreted as necessary, that is,
causal factors. Thereby, causality is removed from objects and
transferred to man, not different from the way this is done by
Kant, when he says that causality is a category of reason. Kant
does not accept, however, Hume's explanation of causality from
the mere experience of the individual. The Kantian formulation,
whereby causality is an a priori of experience, truly points to the
direction of an explanation in greater depth. For the psychological
regularity which Hume has discovered must be supplemented by,
and even justified through, the idea of a spiritual entity, or mind,
endowed with forces or tendencies that appear as aptitudes in the
process of becoming. Physiologically, the differentiation of human
thought from the *consecution des bêtes* can be comprehended already from the nature of the human cerebral cortex, by dint of
which the active coordination of received impressions is necessary,
grows and takes shape, and must be understood as a definite relation between a total configuration of impressions and the particular impressions which occur at a given instance. For the total con-

figuration is the absolute a priori; it can be conceived only as
involving the totality of nature through as yet ill-defined general
relationships, of which some gradually become clearer through the
development and the actions of the brain and the sense organs, that
is, through the comprehending mind of man. Each sequential experience, like any other activity, takes place in a totality configuration and through the organs which belong to that configuration.
However, this results in a *regressus in infinitum*, leading back to
the origins of organic life which, if conceived psychically, might
as well be understood as the incorporation of experience. This
follows from the recognition that every kind of action and of suffering (because suffering is only an aspect of action), or life itself,
is experience, just as experience, in turn, is either action or suffering. Action involves organic change; it leaves tracks of one kind
or another, be it in the same or the opposite direction as the tendency of the growth and development of the organism, or even in-
differently defined. This is what is known as memory. More specifically, memory is the continuing labor and force of sensual
impressions, which are evident in the shape of coordinated complexes, that is, of fixed emotions which are themselves the product
of memory.

Every possible transformation of an organ is, to be sure, conditioned by its nature and by its place in a total configuration, that
is, by the manner in which the organ in question is predisposed
and likely to accept, or not to accept, the change. It is in this sense
that I propose (in the second book of this essay on *Gemeinschaft
und Gesellschaft*) the unity of, as well as the differentiations between, liking, habituation, and memory as elementary modifica-
tions of will and spiritual force in each and every mental production. This proposition extends to the problem of the origin and
the history of human cognition. In other words, all this is merely
an explication, partly following Spinoza and Schopenhauer, and
partly the biological theory of descendence; it is an interpretation
of the idea by means of which Kant has, indeed, overcome Hume.
From the correctness of this interpretation derives not only the
fact that, but also the reason why, we cannot think of what is in
being otherwise than as being in action and of what is becoming

otherwise than as acted upon; these are antecedent, and even eternal, functions which are imprinted in the very structure of our cognitive processes, that is, our power of reasoning. Not to be able to do otherwise is a necessity upon which our feeling of certainty is founded, because being active per se and being active according to one's nature is one and the same thing, in line with the formal rule of identity.

If it is true that human beings form a natural community of thought because causality is within us like sense organs and if, as a consequence, we necessarily attach names to subjects and objects (what is acting and what is acted upon), then whatever differentiates these phenomena can only be the result of thought—thought about what are the subjects that are acting, that is, the truly real entities. Peoples, groups, individuals differ in this regard, even if there is wide agreement that the active principle in nature is expressed in mythological and poetic imagery. Linguistic forms are testimony to that fact. To be sure, the differentiation between dead (that is, only acted upon) phenomena and those that are alive (meaning those that are acting) is an early acquisition of thought; nevertheless, what prevails is the idea that nature is a living thing, that action is voluntary, and that gods and demons participate in it, along with visible subjects. However, if ultimately world and fate are put into the head and the hand of a unitary God who has created them out of nothing, maintained them according to his pleasure, and endowed them with rules and laws according to which whatever happens appears as regularity and necessity, then, all subordinated wills and liberties in nature, including man's own free will, are made to disappear and tendencies that cannot be deduced from received external action are understood only as inexplicable inclinations and forces. In that case, even the *liberum arbitrium indifferentiae* is being reconstructed in the shape of such an inexplicable force and mysterious quality, not so much as a fact of experience but as a necessary assumption which is designed to exonerate the omnipotent and omniscient from the responsibility of having initiated the violation of his own rules and regulations.

This entire mode of looking at things, like the idea of a unitary divine will, already belongs to a manner of thinking which on

principle is opposed to religious faith and folk belief, even if it
continues to bear the vestiges of its origin from these sources.
These principles develop to the point where they are capable of
resting upon themselves and to appear altogether independent of
the opposing principles whence they sprang while, at the same
time, they encounter principles of their own kind that have freely
unfolded themselves in those areas that are the natural domain of
thought. The reference here is to scientific thought. Now, scientific
thought, where it appears first and in undisputed purity, has nothing to do with the causes of phenomena and still less with human
or divine will; it derives from the skills of comparing and measuring quantities, as a generalized auxiliary technique, such as doing
sums, calculating, computing; in other words, as techniques of
separating and combining, dividing and multiplying given quantities. These operations can easily be performed in thought because thought has prepared an orderly system of names and desig-
nations for them, so that no differentiation in the perceived objects
disturbs the thought-induced posing of identical and arbitrarily
combinable units. Insofar as the operation of such a system requires a hold on some objects, the calculator chooses, if possible,
objects that are identical, conveniently calculable, and easily
manageable; if they are not at his disposal, he will construct them
and endow them with the desired qualities. To be sure, one finds
innumerable configurations in nature that resemble each other to
a larger or lesser degree with regard to their perceived qualities, to
the point where they can be designated as equal; and be it further
granted that it is natural to identify them with a name; nevertheless,
the identification becomes artificial and arbitrary inasmuch as
names are consciously formulated, the individual differences not
only neglected but deliberately excluded from consideration and
virtually destroyed for the purpose of creating a usable and as
nearly as possible perfect equality. However, all scientific thought,
like mathematics, must strive for equality to make measurement
possible, the reason being that measurement is to arrive at general
statements and precise relations, of which equality, in turn, serves
as a measuring rod. In this regard, scientific equations are like
measuring rods in such a way that actual relations between actual

objects are comprehended in relation to them. They are serviceable in the economy of thought. What in innumerable actual instances would have to be calculated again and again is being calculated once and for all in an ideally constructed instance and merely
applied subsequently; regarding the ideally constructed instance, all
actual instances are either identical or stand in an ascertainable
relation to it and consequently to each other. In other words, generalized or scientific concepts, statements, and systems may be
compared to tools by means of which we gain knowledge or arrive
at least at assumptions in particular given instances; the procedure is to insert particular names and conditions in lieu of those
of the fictitious and general instances: the procedure of syllogism.
In a variety of ways, this procedure is used in applied science (as
thinking in analogy to the principle of sufficient reason) and in
pure science relative to a system of names (a terminology), which
is represented in its simplest form by a system of numbers (as
thinking in analogy to the principle of identity). For all pure science refers exclusively to constructions of thought (*Gedankendinge*), such as a generalized object or a quantity (for purposes of
pure calculation) or the extensionless point, the straight line, the
plane without depth, the regular bodies, when relations between
spatial phenomena are to be determined. Similarly, imaginary
events in *time* are considered as type-constructs of actual events,
such as the fall of a body in a vacuum whose velocity is calculated
as a unit in space measured in an arbitrarily measured unit of
time, as equal or changeable, according to certain assumptions.
As a rule, the application turns out to be more difficult the more
the merely thinkable general instance differs from observable particular instances, especially as they grow in complexity and irregu-
larity. If separate bodies, through movement, assume momentary
spatial contact, we arrive at the scientific concept of causality as a
quantity of performed labor (contained in movement) which
equals another quantity of labor, namely the effect, and consequently is interchangeable with it, according to the principle of
the identity of action and reaction; this becomes a pure concept
after each and every connotation of reality and productivity has
been eliminated from the concept of force. In some such manner

emerges the great system of pure mechanics; the applications of this system are the concrete natural sciences, especially physics and chemistry.

However, besides and within this scientific view of causality, a philosophical view develops and maintains itself, enhancing as well as critically evaluating the scientific view. It is an organic view as against a mechanical one, a psychological view as against a physical one; according to this view, nothing exists except productive force, the actual and permanent unit of a conservative system of general energy, from which unit all its peculiarities are derived, both as aspects and as effects. All natural laws are serviceable to the principle by means of which the universe is maintained, as all laws that are traceable to mechanics are serviceable to the principle by which the life of an individual or a species is maintained—and it is in individuals and species that "law" becomes reality. The more science, on the one hand, extends its methods to living organisms, the more it must become philosophic in this sense. Conversely, a philosophic view of nature, which would be oriented on the principles of simplicity and necessity, can descend to varied, relative and quasi-accidental truths only to the degree to which it coincides with scientific principles. Such a view must demonstrate life and all its phenomena with the help of type-constructs which are formed in analogy to general ideas, because the derivation of the particular from the general is the essence of life.

All science, and consequently all philosophy as science, is rationalistic. Its objects are things of thought (*Gedankendinge*), that is, constructions. But all philosophy, and consequently all science as philosophy, is empirical, in the sense that to be is to act, existence to be comprehended as movement and the potentiality, probability, necessity of change as the essence of actuality, the nonbeing as the truly being, in brief, dialectically. The empirical and the dialectic methods require and complement each other. Both are concerned with tendencies that meet each other, contest each other, and combine among themselves, which means that they can be understood and become known only as psychological realities. The empirical as well as the dialectic method are confirmed in general and individual psychology because we know that human will is our own will and that human life and fate is a totality consisting of individual wills, the fact that individual wills are always and inexorably conditioned by other natural phenomena notwithstanding. The facts of general psychology are manifested in an actual historical culture or civilization, that is, in human social life and its creations.

History per se, as a collection of facts, is neither science nor philosophy. But history is both science and philosophy to the extent that we are capable of discovering in it the regularities of human existence. History is a totality of events whose beginning and end are accessible only to highly indistinct assumptions. One might say that we are no more in the dark about the future than we are about the past. What we experience as present, we must first observe and attempt to understand. However, a difficulty arises at this point. A large part of the work in this field, whose phenomena are as manifest and as mysterious as those of nature itself, is diminished in its value on account of the difficulty which we encounter in approaching the subject matter in an unbiased way and according to the principles of exact theoretical procedure. The subject, that is, the researcher, is too close to the objects of observation. A great deal of effort and training, perhaps even an innate power of cold reasoning, is required in order to view the phenomena of history with the same remote objectivity with which the natural scientist views the life processes of a plant or an animal. Even a learned and critical public does not, as a rule, desire to learn how, in the view of an author, things are, have become the way they are, and are likely to develop, but rather how, in his opinion, they ought to be; for one is accustomed to observe that one's conception of what ought to be determines one's recognition of what is and has been, and even one's expectation of the future —something which, to a degree, may be unavoidable—but one does not want to admit that the deliberate avoidance of this ever present danger is the very essence of the scientific attitude. One expects and almost demands the point of view and the violent rhetoric of partisanship rather than the imperturbed logic and tranquility of the impartial observer. Consequently, in contemporary social science, and especially in Germany, what is actually a partisan controversy is made to appear as a divergence in pure theory.

One can tolerate such partisanship as a manifestation of opposed tendencies in negotiations relative to legislation and administrative practices, where the representatives of competing interests and social classes, with more or less *bona fides*, may present themselves as advocates of antagonistic convictions and doctrines which in actual fact are nothing but technological principles of politics. Occasionally, divergencies of this sort are deeply rooted in moral sentiments and subjective inclinations; but passions of this or any other kind must not be permitted to disturb the objective evaluation of facts as they are. For example, the weight which is attached to the antagonistic doctrines of individualism and socialism and to their adequacy for the comprehension of what actually occurs in modern industry and commerce appears to me comparable to what would happen if medical practitioners were to transfer allopathic versus homeopathic therapeutic methods to physiology. In view of all this, it would seem important to free onself from all foggy usages of this sort; one must take one's stand outside the phenomena and, as with telescope and microscope, observe structure and processes which inside a culture or civilization are so very different from each other, researchable in general and in large dimensions as in particular and in small dimensions, in the same way as in *natura rerum* the course of heavenly bodies and the life processes of elementary organisms. In the universal view, history is nothing but an aspect of the fate of a planet, that is, a chapter in the development of organic life made possible by the gradual cooling of the earth. In a narrower view, history is the environment and condition of my daily life; it is everything that occurs before my eyes and ears and is known as human action and interaction.

These deliberations are brought to a focus in empirical and dialectic philosophy. The necessities of life, the passions and activities of men are the same empirically and dialectically. The rational disciplines, likewise, refer generally to the same phenomena. These disciplines assume absolutely separate and rationally or arbitrarily acting individuals; they attempt to analyze, on the one hand, the ideally conceived relations and combinations of their wills and, on the other hand, the changes in material conditions that occur by means of commercial contact. The former, attentive to the formal consequences of relations between isolated individuals, is represented by pure jurisprudence or natural law; the latter, devoted to the material aspect of these relations, is represented by political economy; the former may be compared to geometry; the latter to abstract mechanics. Both approaches, if applied to social reality, are all the more fruitful, the more developed and complex human activities and relationships have become in the wake of the advancement of culture. In spite of this, "organic" and "historical" views have been put forward in opposition to both natural law and political economy. The present theory [of *Gemeinschaft* and *Gesellschaft*] attempts to absorb these theories and to keep them in a state of dependence. But in this respect, as in others, the theory has not been able to do more than indicate the variety of approaches rather sketchily. The complexities of the subject matter are overwhelming. The schemata of thought that have been proposed ought to be judged more with regard to their utility than with regard to their correctness. Only further analysis in the future will show how useful the theory really is, and I wish myself strength and encouragement to that effect. I shall not be responsible, though, both for erroneous explications and for presumably clever applications. People who are not trained in conceptual thinking better abstain from passing judgment. However, I am persuaded that such abstention, as well as any other, ought not to be expected in this time and age.

I could write a special chapter about the influences to which I owe the furtherance of my ideas. I could mention a number of them in the field of the social sciences. Some of the more important names are occasionally quoted. I should like to mention, though, that the great sociological works of Comte and Spencer have accompanied me on my way. Both have their weaknesses, the former more in its prehistorical foundations, the latter more in its view of history; both see the evolution of mankind too onesidedly and directly conditioned by man's intellectual progress.

I further ought to mention that I have followed eagerly the efforts of Albert Schaeffle and Adolf Wagner in their important books. However, both of them, in my opinion, have not come up to the profound political insight of Rodbertus regarding the pathology of modern society, which theorists as well as legislators, all good intentions notwithstanding, can do little else but modify. I do not conceal, moreover, that my analysis received lasting impressions—stimulating, informative, and confirming—from the very different works of three excellent authors, Sir Henry Sumner Maine, Otto von Gierke, and Karl Marx. Sir Henry Sumner Maine (*Ancient Law, Village Communities in the East and West, The Early History of Institutions, Early Law and Custom*) is a philosophically trained historian of law with a very wide horizon. It is to be regretted, however, that he puts up an unjustified resistance against the inordinately informative insight with which Bachofen (*Mutterrecht*) and Morgan (*Ancient Society*) have penetrated the prehistory of the family, the community, and institutions in general; Maine's optimistic judgment of modern society I do not hold against him. I have always admired Gierke's erudition (*Das deutsche Genossenschaftsrecht, Johannes Althusius*, etc.) and respected his judgment, although regarding the economistic approach to society, which I consider most important, I have found little in his writings that I could have used in my own work. In this regard, Karl Marx is the most remarkable and profound of the social philosophers (*Critique of Political Economy, Das Kapital*). I am emphasizing Marx all the more eagerly because he has never been forgiven the supposedly utopian fantasy whose definitive refutation was his very pride. The idea which I express the following way: that the natural and for us past and gone, yet always basic, constitution of culture is communistic, the actual and the coming one socialistic, in my opinion, is not foreign to those historians who understand their own work well enough; but only the discoverer of the capitalistic mode of production knew how to make the idea thoroughly clear. I see in all this an interconnectedness of facts which is as natural as life and death. I might find life enjoyable, death regrettable: but joy and sadness are resolved in the contemplation of divine fate. I am altogether unique in my terminology and in my definitions. One thing, however, is easy to comprehend: there is no individualism in history and culture, except as it emanates from *Gemeinschaft* and remains conditioned by it, or as it brings about and sustains *Gesellschaft*. Such contradictory relation of individual man to the whole of mankind constitutes the pure problem.

3

PREFACE TO THE SECOND EDITION OF *GEMEINSCHAFT UND GESELLSCHAFT*

THIS TREATISE, first published twenty-five years ago, has persistently, although slowly, gained a not insignificant influence on the growth of sociological theories in the German language areas and beyond (in Italy, Denmark, Russia, and America). And this has happened in spite of very unfavorable, even adverse, circumstances. The book was meant for philosophers. Although such men as Paulsen and Hoeffding stressed its significance, and even Wundt characterized it as rich in thought—and although Ueberweg-Heinze's and Vorlaender's histories of modern philosophy considered it worth mentioning, contemporary philosophy on the whole remained silent. The new concepts here propounded were not even regarded as worthy of criticism or possible refutation.

The deeper reason for this is the relationship of philosophy to the problems of ethics. There is, to be sure, no lack of books on ethics, and in particular the three heads of the newest philosophical wisdom, whose names were mentioned, happen to have published such books, and they met with great success. These books, of course, did not ignore the problems of contemporary social life or those of the evolutionary history of mankind; they have inquired into these very seriously. Also the publications of Eucken and Barth may be mentioned in this connection.

Yet everyone knows, and knows it as a significant fact, that

Translated from Vorrede zur zweiten Auflage (1912) of *Gemeinschaft und Gesellschaft*, according to the new edition (Darmstadt: Wissenschaftliche Buchgesellschaft, 1963), pp. xxvi–xxxviii. The last two paragraphs have been omitted.

sociology is not accepted at German universities, even at a side table of philosophy; sociology is deliberately excluded from its symposia.

The cause of this exclusion is not a dislike of the name which, in fact, is used more and more by philosophers. It is an aversion to the subject; philosophy, especially the leading academic philosophy, does not feel equal to a thorough and radical treatment of these problems. The reasons for this sentiment are more than accidental.

The growth of modern philosophy has been closely bound up with the growth of the natural sciences. Two hundred years ago the Aristotelian scholastic philosophy with the corresponding theological doctrine of morality, law, and society still prevailed. The eighteenth century brought modernization, at least in Protestant Germany, as did the Revolution in France: the universities followed the bourgeois movement and its political progress.

In addition, the philosophy which attached itself to the mechanistic conception of nature included a doctrine of law and a theory of society, which, in fact, were considered the principal elements of ethics. The tendency of this "practical" philosophy was of necessity antitheological, antifeudal, antimedieval. It was individualistic and therefore, according to my terminology, associational rather than communal in nature.

The great and historically significant contributions of this philosophy are the rationalistic, "natural rights" theory of law and the "political economy" of the physiocratic school which is intimately connected with it. The latter was continued by the "classical" English school of political economy. In the preface to the first edition of this treatise I compared the former to geometry and the latter to abstract mechanics.

Both the doctrine of natural law and political economy contributed greatly to the formation of the rapidly developing modern society and the corresponding rapid growth of the modern state. Both developments took place under the banner of revolution— the great French Revolution, which destroyed the Holy Roman Empire, and the smaller revolutions which followed in France and Germany—here partly through the action of the Prussian monarchy, which was revolutionary in origin and drive; these revolutions, which continued throughout the nineteenth century, provided powerful impulses to capitalism and to a legislation which essentially served the purpose of capitalism.

All revolutions, however, evoke powerful countermovements; restorations and reactionary tendencies follow these repercussions with evident necessity.

The "restoration of the political sciences"—a designation which includes the historical school of jurisprudence—wanted to finish off the natural-rights doctrine and, above all, the rational and individualistic construction of the state as a contract. It succeeded in doing so, at least in Germany—particularly as regards the "academic" representation of these doctrines. For in England, the theory of legislation and the analytical jurisprudence of Bentham and Austin deliberately reverted to Thomas Hobbes. In the Latin countries, in Russia, and in America, the natural-rights doctrine continued more or less to be acknowledged as the liberal philosophy of law.

But even in Germany, the philosophy of law was not altogether neglected although it receded to the background as an academic discipline. The historical school which was initiated by the skeptic Hugo and the Catholic romanticist Savigny, as well as by the Protestant-conservative system of Stahl, who was of Jewish descent, reverted to Schelling's originally pantheistic but increasingly fantastic philosophy of nature. Also the philosophy of law of Krause and his more successful disciple Ahrens was pantheistic, although with a somewhat more humanitarian, cosmopolitan, Masonic bent. But the philosophy of Hegel had a much earlier and more powerful impact, even in developing and adapting Schelling's thoughts: in natural law, as expressed in "The Philosophy of Right" (1820), Hegel intends to unfold the nature of the objective spirit which, starting from free will, posits its abstract object in the law and rises to morality, the idea of which assumes reality in the state.

What made this system significant was that it undertook to conceive the modern social structures—society and the state—as spiritual-natural entities. That is, to demonstrate them as necessary, instead of simply rejecting them as being based on theoretical errors, as was the inherent tendency of romanticism and historical jurisprudence and, indeed, restorative and reactionary thought. On the other hand, in the Hegelian system—its reference to "world history" notwithstanding—all historical insight, as well as any theory of real relationship between individual will and social groups, is blotted out. Hegel's philosophy of right is not only an interpretation and construction but also a glorification of the state, and for him the state which realizes the moral idea is the existing state, that is, the Prussian state of the Restoration period which, however, cannot altogether deny its radical past. Hegel's theory of the state, therefore, is as ambiguous as this conservative absolutism; its ambiguousnes became evident in the Hegelian school of thought. The Hegelian left wing led from the officially approved, quasi-absolutist, liberalism to democratic liberalism and beyond, yet without academic acceptance.

Parallel with the decline of Hegel's philosophy runs the replacement of the old Prussian concept of the state—cloaked in the conservative *Deutsche Bund*—by the idea of German unification, which Prussian thought for a long time had held in scorn; paradoxically, as with so many historical fulfillments, it came about in such a way that the idea of the Prussian state became its forceful tool.

During this epoch philosophy lost the spiritual, that is, the ethical-political leadership of the German nation. Its fate was the fate of a liberalism, which by the epithet "national" indirectly expressed that it had chosen subordination in principle and that it considered itself less called upon to lead the more radical elements than to adjust to the reactionary ones.

This mentality remained in contact with enlightenment only in the area of the natural sciences, but even this only to the extent that it carefully avoided conflicts with official religiosity. This was especially true after 1878, when the struggle between the state and the Roman Catholic Church (*Kulturkampf*) had been abandoned and a tolerant-friendly relationship even to the papal church had been made an article of the national creed.

The deeper-lying connections with the general social development are easily discernible. The development of large-scale industry had started in Germany after 1840, in constant interaction with the neighboring countries, France and England; the labor movement and with it the socialistic-communistic doctrines knocked at the gates.

They knocked also at the gates of the universities. Economics predominantly was a practical political doctrine. It had essentially supported capitalism and free competition. "Laissez-faire" was its slogan. To be sure, German scholarship attempted to attribute to political economy a historical character and thus contributed to breaking the dogmatism of the Manchester school. Ethical motivations spoke strongly in favor of the struggling working class. Academic socialism (*Katheder-Sozialismus*) entered the stage. The name had not been invented by its supporters, but they felt confident enough to adopt it. Political economy, which had already, in England, incurred the odium of materialism—through the passionate eloquence of Carlyle and Ruskin's ethically and aesthetically tinged accusations—now appeared in the garb of German idealism, which considered it fitting to appeal primarily to the sense of duty of the propertied classes.

Foremost among the men who thus created a new social-political consciousness were scholars like Schmoller, Brentano, Knapp, each of them active and influential in his particular way. Adolf Wagner and Albert Schaeffle asserted with considerable success the demand for methodical strictness and systematic generalization in the great controversy of socialism versus capitalism (or individualism). Wagner, under the influence of a genuine socialist (Rodbertus), pleaded for the extension of governmental action, for the legal theory of all private property, for the predominance of social economic over private economic concepts. Schaeffle ventured upon a description of "The Structure and Life of the Social Organism" (*Bau und Leben des Sozialen Koerpers*) in a similar spirit, but with greater philosophical ambition. He agrees with Herbert Spencer—in fact he was strongly influenced by him—in the "organicistic" interpretation of sociology. But whereas Spencer arrived at the postulate of an administrative nihilism, Schaeffle advocated administrative universalism. Yet, both conceived of the development of civilization in the light of the evolution of all life, that is, of descendence theory, drawing conclusions which, although perhaps irrefutable in their basic elements, soon carry the mind onto the slippery ice of assumptions which hover between fear and hope. Auguste Comte, on the other hand, intended to establish sociology on a positivistic foundation, by deducing the definitive and correct structure of social life and politics from a definitive and correct theory, according to the law of evolution of human thought, the law of the three stages. A certain relationship to Hegelian dialectics is unmistakable in this. Generally, the idea of a creative synthesis of the practical tendencies of the time characterized progressive thought in the nineteenth century.

Ever since the seventeenth century, all enlightened scholars had adhered to the notion of an evolution of civilization from barbarism and savagery and of men from brutelike conditions, replacing the belief in paradisiacal origins and glories. This approach had been obscured by Restoration and romanticism and consequently had to be regained through Darwinism; yet, essentially, the approach is not so much an application of a biological theory of evolution as the latter is a generalization from it. In Hegel and Comte this essential independence from the biological theory is still clearly evident.

What distinguishes Comte is that, under the powerful influence of Saint-Simon, he takes a critical position toward progress, modernity, and liberalism. The romanticists, the defenders of tradition, of the Middle Ages, and of authority, did the same. But Saint-Simon and Comte take this position on the basis of progress, of modernity, and of liberalism. Without wanting to return to faith and to feudalism, they recognize the prevalence of a positive and organic order during the Middle Ages, and they likewise recognize the essentially negative and revolutionary character of modernity without repudiating science, enlightenment, and freedom but, on the contrary, affirming and emphasizing these all the more.

Such is also the inevitable position of socialist theories toward the problems of culture. A socialist theory, in this context, does not mean a theory making certain value judgments about capitalism, private property, and the proletariat and postulating a certain policy or even a new social order. Socialism in this sense merely means a theory which does not simply validate the implicit and accepted value judgments of liberalism and of the dominant view in social philosophy but places itself outside and above the contrast to which this view, without realizing it, remains naïvely confined.

Socialist theory takes a critical position toward things as they are and their development; that is, as a theory, it is primarily cognitive, contemplating, observing.

Herein lies the permanent significance of the *Critique of Political Economy*. For political economy in its classical form, which is retained even in its historical-ethical modification, meant to describe and establish the allegedly normal social organization, that is, one that is based on individual liberty and equality of acquired rights. In other words, it is based on the unlimited inequality of property and on the cleavage of society in the class of propertied owners, on the one hand, and that of the proletariat, on the other.

In contrast to these assumptions, the following insights are fundamentally important: (1) that most of traditional culture has existed and flourished without these allegedly normal conditions, as without railroads, telegraphs, and automatic devices; that, on the contrary, common property by all the people, at least of the land, and private property of the means of production by industrial laborers has been the rule historically, and to a large extent they still are; (2) that even "present society is not a solid crystal but an organism, capable of change and constantly in a process of change." (Karl Marx, *Das Kapital*, preface to the first edition, July 25, 1867).

Furthermore, it is an indispensable element of "scientific socialism" that political conditions, or even the scientific, artistic, and ethical tendencies, are not primarily the initiating factors of social movements, no matter how much they may be coeffective; rather, the initating factors are the crude material needs, sensations, and feelings of the workaday life which are differentiated by social conditions, and therefore shape up differently in different strata and classes; this relatively independent variable has a definite effect upon political conditions and cultural trends, even if, in turn, it is constantly promoted or retarded and always significantly modified by their influences.

Ethnological and sociological research ("from Bachofen to Morgan," as I put it in the preface of this treatise in 1887) and furthermore the rivers and rivulets of economic and legal history had combined in the direction indicated under (1). This is why I turned with rapt attention to the enlightening lectures of Henry Maine, and why I was infinitely enriched by Gierke's *Genossenschaftsrecht*, a work in which he subjects the legal as well as the cultural economic, social, and ethical aspects of cooperative institutions to a learned and profound analysis in order to explain the formation of law and to demonstrate the indissoluble relationship between law and culture.

More closely connected with my special studies was the same author's *Althusius*, through its discussion of the theories of the state that are based on natural law. For I had taken my departure from Hobbes, to whose biography and philosophy I had devoted diligent studies in the years 1877 to 1882. I owe the stimulation for these studies to Paulsen[1]; with Paulsen and with all those who know and have studied that great thinker, I admire the energy and consistency of the Hobbesian construction of the state. However, when I traced the powerful influence of Hobbesian concepts in England and elsewhere, down to the nineteenth century, I was astounded by the decline of this rationalistic and individualistic philosophy of law, which in the eighteenth century had been accepted as the pinnacle of wisdom. Really, should theories be considered worthless and meaningless, the core of which had been accepted as correct by men like Kant, Fichte, Feuerbach; theories which had been basic for all of modern legislation, for the emancipation of the peasants as for freedom of trade, by their influence on political economy and administration; theories which had been

[1]   Friedrich Paulsen, like Toennies of Frisian descent, professor of philosophy and education at the University of Berlin, was until his death in 1908 connected with Toennies in intimate friendship; cf. Olaf Klose, E. G. Jacoby, Irma Fischer, *Ferdinand Toennies-Friedrich Paulsen, Briefwechsel 1876–1908* (Kiel: F. Hirt, 1961).—Eds.

basic to the system of Bentham, so influential in England and beyond?

The void created by the elimination of the doctrines of natural law and its political philosophy had been filled by historical jurisprudence, the organic theory of the state, and a groping eclecticism, in which again and again theology emerges as the most self-assured element, and one that could be certain of the acclaim of the powers that be.

The theological foundation of law and social corporations (*Verbaende*) is historically highly significant, but otherwise scientific thinking is concerned about it only because it has to overcome it. The purely historical view operates without concepts and is therefore not knowledge in a philosophical sense. The only debatable theory of this kind is the theory of the "organic" nature of law and the state, which has been connected with theology since ancient times. Recently it has reappeared, partly in connection with the philosophy of nature to which theology soon reasserts its relationship (Stahl), but partly also in the new garb of biological analogy. This is a reciprocal matter: biology aims to explain and interpret the natural organism by means of comparison with the facts of social life, as sociology does in converse fashion with regard to "social organisms."

I never denied that some analogies of this kind are well founded. They result from phenomena which are general and common to all life, as unity in diversity, as the interaction of parts with each other and of these parts with the whole, that is, the tendencies which we recognize and designate, on the one hand, as differentiation of organs and functions, on the other hand, as the division of labor.

However, I never could make sense out of the assertion that the state, the local community, or any human cooperative "is" an organism, even if a man like Gierke affirms this conception with the whole weight of his idealism; he did it as late as 1902 in an excellent lecture on "The Nature of Human Corporations." External and internal experience, he says, suggest the assumption of effective corporative units; he adds that some of the impulses which determine our actions originate from the communities (*Gemein-*

schaften) penetrating our individual selves; that the certainty with which we feel that our self is real comprises the fact that we are subunits of more complex life units, even if we may not find these in our consciousness and can infer only indirectly, from the effects of the community within us, that social wholes are of a physical-mental nature. Consequently, Gierke assumes that the law of human corporations represents an existential system for socially determined living beings, comprising the entirety of social law, with the legal concepts of constitution, membership, juridical person, executive organ, and the act of free will, all of which creates a corporate personality—and this not by way of contract, but as a creative act of the community.

In contrast to this, I make a stricter distinction between natural corporations, the significance of which for social life is indeed eminent, and cultural or artificial units, although the latter may proceed from the former.

To be sure, the former, too, exist *in* and *for* our consciousness, but not essentially *by* our consciousness, as do the properly and truly social relationships and associations. For I claim this insight to be the fundamental sociological insight: that, aside from the real units and relationships between men, there exist units and relationships posited by and depending upon their own will, and therefore essentially of an ideally conceived character. They must be understood as created or made by men, even though, in fact, they may have attained an external objective power over the individual, a power which always is and means the power of united wills over single wills.

I saw the great meaning of rational natural law in the fact that it attempted to comprehend anthropologically the entities which so far had been interpreted predominantly in a theological manner, explaining these seemingly supernatural structures as creations (*Gebilde*) of human thought and will.

Yet I never doubted that this was not an explanation of general validity. The historical school of jurisprudence, whose favorite was the common law, and which appealed to the natural sense of justice and the quietly working forces of the folk culture (*Volksgeist*), had at that time received many new confirmations

by the extensive studies of primitive agrarian communism which
—after von Maurer, Haxthausen, and others—just then were combined by Laveleye. Other endorsements came from the interpretation of the legal structures of clans and families, whose basic
features, similarities as well as differences, were presented by com-
parative jurisprudence. Especially, the elements of the Aryan institutions became visible and transparent. Leist's fine works dug
deeply into the problem, to my intense satisfaction; prior to that,
The Aryan Household, by the Australian Hearne, had made a
great impression on me. Also the writings of Post were useful to
me; Lyall's *Asiatic Studies* introduced me to the still alive Indian
clan and informed me about the relation between state and religion in China. With this was combined the profound impression
of Fustel de Coulanges' *La Cité antique*, Bachofen's *Mutterrecht*,
Morgan's *Ancient Society*, and others.

All these works furthered and deepened the insight into the
distinguishing features of modern society and the modern state,
which concepts I had found propounded with absolute validity in
Lorenz von Stein's significant analysis. Added to this was the new
theory of society, which R. von Jhering outlined in his unfortu-
nately fragmentary *Zweck im Recht*; (vol. I, 1877), a work proceeding in wholly rationalistic fashion, so that this work appeared
to me as a "renewal of the natural rights doctrine." I also considered A. Wagner's profound discourses on the philosophy of law
(in his *Grundlegung*, vol. 1, 1876) as such a renewal despite (or
because of) their state-socialistic tendencies. Already at that time
I shared that approach to practical policy, but the theoretical construction did not appear to me satisfactory in every respect.

The idea of writing the present book began to mature when in
1880 I came across a passage in Maine's *Ancient Law*, which I
have quoted in German (cf. Loomis' translation, p. 182). The
contract is there described as the typical legal transaction and as
characteristic for all rational legal relationships and these, again,
as the confirmed expressions of all rationally conceived social relationships; consequently, then, society and the state have likewise
to be conceived as contracts between individuals, that is, as based
on their free and conscious will. However, not all legal relation-

ships and corporations can be construed according to this formula, especially not the initial and continually effective familial ones. Are they nothing but enforced ("military") relations, as they appeared to Herbert Spencer? Obviously not. They, too, are affirmed by free will, even though not in the same manner as those relationships and agreements which are clearly and distinctly conceived as means for the complementary and coinciding purposes of the individuals. In which way? That was now my problem.

From here originated the theorem of *Gemeinschaft* and *Gesellschaft* and, inseparable from it, that of essential will and arbitrary will. Two types of social relationships—two types of the formation of individual wills—but both to be derived from one and the same point of departure, namely, the relation between the whole and its parts, the ancient Aristotelian contrast of organism and artifact in which, however, the artifact itself ought to be understood as in its essence more or less related either to the organic or the mechanical aggregate. All social forms are artifacts of psychic substance, and their sociological conceptualization, therefore, must be a psychological conceptualization at the same time.

Hoeffding, himself a psychologist with a bent toward sociology, attracted to it by his interest in ethics and the philosophy of religion, wrote about this book that it combined sociology and psychology in a unique way by showing how social development is essentially connected with, and has its counterpart in, a corresponding evolution of human mental faculties.[2] Wundt, who also considered these concepts worth mentioning, supposes that my distinctions of the forms of will probably correspond to "the more common one of simple or instinctual will and composite will or choice."[3] My answer (*Archiv fuer systematische Philosophie* IV, vol. 4, pp. 487 f.) was:

For me, instinctual will is only the germinal form of essential will; the latter comprises not only composite will of the most complicated kinds, but essential will unfolds and realizes its nature as *human* will only through composite will; for I never have called the "natural in-

2   Mindre Arbejder, p. 144, Copenhagen, 1899.
3   Logik II,[2] p. 599.

stincts" of men their will; rather, I conceive human will always as *appetitus rationalis*. As *appetitus*, moreover, I conceive not so much the urge (or resistance) to do something as the positive or negative attitude to the object (the *Nicht-Ich*), which forms the basis of the urge to act; this relation becomes essential will only if it is accompanied and coeffected by thought. I repeat: essential will is realized only in the composite will—for I thus interpret the whole realm of ideas of a creative personality, such as an artist or ethical genius, namely, as the expression of his essential will. But I thus interpret as will every free act, inasmuch as it evolves from the essential tendencies of the actor's mind, feeling, or conscience. Therefore: by essential will in its social determination and by *Gemeinschaft* I understand and analyze what Hegel calls the concrete substance of the *Volksgeist*, something rising so far beyond the "social instincts" that, in fact, it determines and supports the whole culture of a people.

Political economy largely leads its own life, apart from philosophy. Yet, political economy always has been searching for a relation to philosophy and often has vividly expressed the desire for a philosophical foundation. During the twenty-five years which have gone by since the publication of this book, this has become more evident than ever before. Pure sociology slowly has been raised to the rank of an auxiliary science of political economy, as was visibly documented by the founding of sociological associations in which economists have taken a leading part.

The concepts of social life, here submitted, although entirely new in their formulation, could not strike the economists as altogether strange. They were prepared for them by the contrast, with which they were familiar, between household economy (*oikos*) and money economy and some related concepts. The two leaders in German social science, Schmoller and Wagner, have both concerned themselves with this treatise, although from very different methodological viewpoints. Rationalism and the rational mechanization of production, indeed of the "world," increasingly have been recognized as the distinguishing traits of the whole modern epoch, and they have been expounded as such in several important investigations.

4

NORMAL CONCEPTS

EDITORS' NOTE. *This chapter makes it evident that Max Weber's elaboration of the ideal type as a conceptual image of essential reality has been anticipated by Toennies, both in his work on Hobbes and in passages from* Gemeinschaft und Gesellschaft *that commonly receive only a fleeting glance from the reader, if indeed they are read at all. In addition, Toennies' contention that thinking in "normal concepts," or ideal-typical thinking, is already contained in the writings of Hobbes makes it imperative to go beyond the classical economists and the Scottish moralists—not to mention Auguste Comte—in the search for the roots of sociological reasoning as we know it today.*

Two passages from Toennies' highly significant book on the life and work of Thomas Hobbes are followed by two passages from Gemeinschaft und Gesellschaft. *If seen together, they will make Toennies' position entirely clear.*

An additional piece about "Hobbes and the Zoon Politikon" *develops the concept of* Gesellschaft *out of the philosophy of Hobbes; the paper on "The Concept of* Gemeinschaft" *may be considered a companion piece.*

The Formation of Modern Theory

THE REAL significance of the philosophical disputes at the beginning of the modern epoch is the passing of the Christian world view and the rise of a new one, which seeks its basis in sci-

Translated from *Thomas Hobbes, Leben und Lehre*, 3d ed. (Stuttgart: Frommann Verlag, 1925), pp. 86–90. Statements on pp. 87–88 have been slightly abbreviated. Subtitles supplied by the editors.

entific understanding, instead of in faith, but for that very reason finds itself in opposition to all opinions that are held to be natural, traditional, and sacred.

The general character of the social change underlying these conflicts can be grasped by three criteria. The first is that the direction of aims and activities is one from the internal to the external. The second, closely related to the first, is a transition from relative rest to increased motion in greater freedom. And third, the whole spirit of the age and its outstanding thought is a progress from practice and art to theory and science.

For their relationship is that of motion to rest. Theory is motor power, destroying and building. Gradually developed out of practice yet remaining dependent on it, theory tends to become absolute and achieves a dominant position. Practice and art are firmly bound to tradition; with regard to them, thought is subject to authority and remains dogmatic, in agreement with the unlearned folk, to whom simplicity is second nature, the extant venerable, valid doctrine sacred. Theory and science search for what is new, think freely and critically, set themselves apart from common habits of thought, make everything equally an object of inquiry, fight persistence in the traditional ways, which turn as in a circle, and thus boldly progress in a straight line.

The transition from rounded restrictedness to the establishment of distant contacts, and thus, as it were, from the closed circular line to the infinite straight line, from the organic to the mechanical motion, characterizes the nature of the general economic development in this modern period. It provides for enlarged areas of commerce; subjects their inhabitants to the same laws, the same system of weights and measures, the same currency; makes the state, that is, the absolute government, the sole judge and master, who executes the administration of its own legislation as though by mechanical force. Like economic development, the state acts against folkways and all traditional authorities, hence also against the Church, whenever it keeps in line with its own motive power and its own conception. The state promotes the monetary economy, which it needs for its financial requirements and the augmentation of its power; the state, therefore, promotes not only commerce and manufacture but the sciences, which open up the treasures of the earth and set free the productivity of labor. To improve weapons technology and tooling for the construction of bridges, fortresses, and roads is the immediate aim of the state as the master of the armed establishment. As the highest judicial authority, it is clearly the concern of the state to act so that legislation be uniform, plain, and lucid, jurisdiction rapid and secure, and law and administration of justice commensurate to actual circumstances, that is, conceived rationally; its concern is to protect the life, property, and honor of everyone against everyone.

These effects of political action are fully analogous to the general social implications of the new development. Within both the political and the social systems arise the unprejudiced, even unscrupulous, rational-willed individual members of society, who aspire to power and make use of every available means for their own ends. As they are made, so they act: individual men, groups, states get more sharply differentiated, engage in competition, learn how to calculate more recklessly their own gain. It is between and beside these social actors that now steps the thinker, enlightened and spreading enlightenment. His activity, too, is one of sharp and clear distinction and combination, in its purest form calculation (arithmetic), and mathematics generally. He, too, turns from the internal to the external, from contemplation of his own self, his salvation, and his faith toward the external world, which no longer is a mere expedient but becomes a truly real object of understanding and knowledge. What the thinker perceives in the external world is no longer a state of rest as its natural condition because it was the godly and blessed condition of fulfillment: what he perceives now is nothing but motion. He analyzes the curve by a set of straight lines that are moving and of varied direction, just as he endeavors to analyze all data by their single component elements, so that what was obscure is rendered lucid, and what was confused can be sorted out. He no longer asks the purpose of things but inquires into the effective cause of all changes in location. He eliminates the variations that are due to differences in language and creed, and tries as much as possible to re-create all phenomena by their common factors. Thus he construes the mutual rights of individuals, who by origin are equal, as spheres of power established by common consent; he construes the state as the personification of this common will, which, at the same time, is an individual will.

What we here mark off conceptually is never found complete and pure in reality. But here, as elsewhere, we will have to understand reality in a first approximation and with the greatest clarity through ideally conceived schemata. The next step is to inquire into the transitions, and then into the constraints and complications.

The transitions are as fluid and varied as application and extension of rational thought are natural and necessary. Not until this method is freely used and constantly improved to reach fullest mastery are the relevant contrasts revealed.

The Logic of the Social Sciences

"I know (said Hobbes in the dedicatory letter of *De Corpore*) that that part of philosophy, wherein are considered lines and figures, has been delivered to us notably improved by the ancients; and withal a most perfect pattern of the logic by which they were enabled to find out and demonstrate such excellent theorems as they have done. . . ." Despite this acknowledgment, one cannot deny that the logic of Hobbes has some original traits. That famous dispute that arose over the logic of Aristotle: whether the universals, that is to say, concepts, or more exactly their objects, exist in the things or only in our thinking about them, is dismissed briefly. The most rigorous nominalism is to his way of thinking self-evident. Things exist naturally as single objects. We collect them, by giving them names according to their common criteria. We connect names in statements, and a statement is true whenever two names are in fact names of the same thing. Whether they are such depends on man's will, first of all on the will, or intention, of the speaker. But when many use the same name or (which comes to the same) the same language, they must be agreed about the use of names. This is particularly necessary in science, for science consists in exactly true statements. Every science must therefore start with definitions, that is, fixing the names to be used, which is an essentially arbitrary action. One may quarrel about the serviceability of a definition; its truth cannot be called in question. It is true and right for him who has made it and who, to be sure, is presumed to know what it is that he defines. If he decides and declares: this be A, that be named B, he must know the this and that,

---

Translated from *Thomas Hobbes, Leben und Lehre*, 3d ed. (Stuttgart: Frommann Verlag, 1925), pp. 111–14.

In an amending note to the 3d ed. Toennies elaborated on the text translated here. The first part of this note reads as follows: "The most important advance in Hobbes' theory of knowedge was that (1) his (nominalist) opinion that truth rested entirely on the combination of names and that names were arbitrary and by agreement, led him forth to (2) the insight that demonstrable truth exists only as regards those objects that we ourselves construe and create, and that in the definition of the names of such objects their origin and cause must be expressed."

whether by sense perception, or by a mere notion, or, finally, solely by a consciously conceived fiction; in one way or another he must have it before him in his mind. Hence also he who wants to converse with him.

This granted, the way the definitive names have been designed does not matter. They are nothing more than appointed signs, their value does not lie in them but in their being appointed, that is, in a clearly conscious and, as it were, contractual agreement. A thinker may settle for such signs only for himself, for his own use, just as much as several persons may settle for them for common use. But whoever wishes to be instructed must accept the definitions given him by his teacher, and he is at liberty only to examine the consistency of the conclusions, that is, of the connections between definitions and the statements derived from them.

"Thinking is computation"—all mental operations can be reduced to addition and subtraction. The nature of thought activity is not different from the combination and dissolution of images as they occur, when an object at first is recognized at a distance in vague outline, then on approach more distinctly, or, conversely, when it gradually loses its characteristic features as it disappears from view. The former is essentially the same as addition, the latter the same as subtraction.

It is a matter of regret that our philosopher, from these sound points of departure, did not penetrate more deeply into the nature of the thought process.

But in order to know something, it is necessary not only to be familiar with a true statement but to comprehend its content, that is, to recall what the names signify, to relate them to an object as well as to the impression one has of that object, since the name, if it is to make sense, must signify that impression. Scientific knowledge, for which these criteria are essential, is therefore in the last analysis based on experience and recall, just as in common knowledge with regard to facts, of which an animal also is capable. As the animal, so the human being learns by experience, which means to imagine a past event and to expect a future event. The human being, however, in doing so has the support of the system of names or language. Language is fixation in memory.

Science is, differently from all knowledge of facts, knowledge of the cause or of the origin of facts. Science, in the specific sense of a priori demonstrability, then, is possible only of the objects we understand and know for certain. If their causation is not contained in the definitions themselves, it cannot be extracted by a derivative statement. Known to us in this specific way, then, is only the origin of those objects that we make ourselves, "whose generation depends on the discretion of man himself." Objects of this kind are geometric figures, because the causes of their properties are contained in the lines drawn by us. Such objects also are right and wrong, equity and injury, "because we ourselves have created their principles, that is, laws and contracts" (*De Hom,* chap. X, 4, 5).

This is the final solution by Hobbes of a problem that deeply concerned him for a long time. He does not penetrate into the last depths of the theory of knowledge. And even at this final point he is still wrestling to give his ideas a different shape from the solution he came up with. What he was really after was the idea that pure science is possible only of pure objects of thought (*Gedankendinge*)—abstract objects and ideally conceived (*ideelle*), events—therefore also of a "body politic," which is not subject to sense perception but whose type we construct. All such objects of thought, pure and simple, are made by us, by sheer ratiocination. And those, of which we assume that they belong to the external and physical world, can in that reality be represented in a more or less perfect fashion. But what we can always do is to measure the facts of reality by those ideas of ours, even when they exist, like the state, only in our thoughts.

If such pure science is restricted to geometry and politics, as in that last-mentioned procedure, it is indeed relatively easily possible to explain the relationship, although this is somewhat more difficult in the field of politics than in geometry. But what remains problematic, because it no more than approaches the causation of real processes, is what Hobbes also demonstrates a priori in his system, namely kinematics, or the theory of motion. A discussion of this problem must be postponed to the chapter on physics.

Normal Concepts and Deviations Therefrom

The concepts of the forms and configurations of will, by and for themselves, are nothing but artifacts of thought, tools devised to facilitate the comprehension of reality. The highly variegated quality of human willing is made comparable by relating it —under the dual aspect of real and imaginary will—to these normal concepts as common denominators.

As free and arbitrary products of thought, normal concepts are mutually exclusive: in a purely formal way nothing pertaining to arbitrary will must be thought into essential will, nothing of essential will into arbitrary will. It is entirely different if these concepts are considered empirically. In this case, they are nothing else but names comprising and denoting a multiplicity of observations or ideas; their content will decrease with the range of the phenomena covered. In this case, observation and deliberation will show that no essential will can ever occur without the arbitrary will by means of which it is expressed and no arbitrary will without the essential will on which it is based. But the strict distinction between normal concepts enables us to discern the existing tendencies toward the one or the other. They exist and take effect alongside each other, they further and augment each other, but, on the other hand, to the extent that each aspires to power and control, they will necessarily collide with each other, contradict and oppose each other. For their content, expressed in norms and rules of behavior, is comparable. Consequently, if arbitrary will desires to order and define everything in accordance with end, purpose or utility, it must overcome the given, traditional, deeply rooted rules insofar as they cannot be adapted to those ends and purposes; or must subordinate them, if that is possible. Therefore, the more decisive arbitrary will or purposeful thinking becomes and the more it concentrates on the knowledge, acquisition, and application of means, to that extent will the emotional and thought complexes which make out the individual

Translated from *Gemeinschaft und Gesellschaft*, new ed. (Darmstadt, 1963), pp. 133–34 (Loomis, pp. 141–42). The translation, on the whole, follows the one by Loomis, but deviates from it in a number of instances.

character of essential will be exposed to the danger of withering away. And not only this, but there also exists a direct antagonism because essential will restrains arbitrary will, resists its freedom of expression and its possible dominance, whereas arbitrary will strives first to free itself from essential will and then attempts to dissolve, destroy, and dominate it. These relations become evident most easily if we take neutral empirical concepts to investigate such tendencies: concepts of human nature and psychological disposition which is conceived as corresponding to and underlying actual and, under certain conditions, regular behavior. Such general disposition may be more favorable either to essential or to arbitrary will. Elements of both may meet and blend in such a general disposition, and one or another may determine its character to a lesser or larger degree.

The Imagination of Types

It is form, not matter, that is enduring. In this regard, the forms of social structure and the forms of essential will are of the same kind; neither can be perceived by the senses or conceived in material categories. The form, as a whole, is always constituted by its elements, which in relation to the form are of material character and maintain and propagate themselves through this very relationship. Thus, for a whole (as enduring form) each of its parts will always be a transitory modification of itself, expressing the nature of the whole in a more or less complete manner. The part could be considered a means to the end of sustaining the whole if at the same time and while it lasted it were not, indeed, an end in itself. At any rate, the parts are similar insofar as they participate in the life of the whole, but different and manifold insofar as each one expresses itself and has a specific function. The same relation exists between a genus (*Realbegriff*) and the groups and individuals that belong to it. This is also true of the relation between individuals and every actual group encompassing them, which must be conceived as being in the process of becoming or declining or in transition to a higher form, always active, alive and changing.

Consequently, what we are taking our departure from is the *essentia* of man, not an abstraction, but the concretely imagined concept of humanity as a whole as the most generally existing reality of this kind. The next steps lead to the *essentia* of race, ethnic group, tribe, and smaller organized groupings and finally to the individual who, as it were, is the centerpiece of these many concentric circles. The more narrowing the lines of the circles which bridge the gap to him, the better is the individual understood. The intuitive and entirely mental recognition of such a whole can be facilitated and more readily grasped by the senses through the imagination (*Vorstellung*) of types each of which must be con-

Translated from *Gemeinschaft und Gesellschaft* (Darmstadt, 1963), pp. 173–74 (Loomis, pp. 171–73). Translation adapted from Loomis, but deviating occasionally. Subtitle supplied.

ceived as comprising the characteristic traits of all the specific manifestations that belong to them prior to their differentiation. Thus, the types are more nearly perfect than the specific manifestations because they embody also those forces and latent capacities which have withered away through lack of use. But, on the other hand, they are more imperfect because they lack the specific qualities which have been developed in reality. For the theory, the concrete but nevertheless constructed image of such a typical entity and its description represents the intellectual idea of the real essence of this meta-empirical whole. In actual life, however, the fullness of the spirit as well as the force of such a whole, can impart itself to its parts only through the natural gathering of the real living bodies in all their initial and actual concreteness; but it may also be conceived as embodied by selected representatives, or even by a single individual who stands for the will and existence of the collectivity.

Hobbes and the Zoon Politikon

The problem. In my monograph on Hobbes I drew attention to several points suggesting the gradual development of his famous political theory, as presented in the three consecutive works: *The Elements of Law Natural and Politic,*[1] *De Cive* (or *The Citizen*), and *Leviathan.*[2] Long before that, my *Notes on the Philosophy of Hobbes* had outlined certain aspects, which I still maintain are essential in the development of Hobbes' thinking. But on neither occasion did I examine the basis of the system of natural law, of which Otto v. Gierke[3] said that it was destined to shatter the traditional natural law doctrine. This explosive element is wrapped in the often repeated thesis that the natural condition of man was a state of war between men; Hobbes calls this, with an expression he did not invent but rendered classic, the war of all against all, while until then (as Gierke puts it) the traditional idea was that of an original community in peace and law. This traditional view fitted well with the thesis of the ancient philosopher that by nature man was an organism designed for the *polis*, that he was a *zoon politikon.* In the *Elements of Law* Hobbes did not mention this theorem. The first chapter of the second edition of *De Cive* (1646), however, which otherwise reproduces the argument of chapter 14 of the *Elements*, has in its second section a paragraph inserted, where Hobbes sets out to refute the doctrine of the *zoon politikon.*[4]

Translated from "Hobbes und das *Zoon Politikon,*" *Zeitschrift fuer Voelkerrecht* 12 (1923) : 471–88; slightly abridged. This paper appeared two years before Toennies issued the third edition of his monograph on Hobbes. References to the monograph have been changed to the third edition. The quotations Toennies selected and translated from Hobbes' writings are given in the original, although in modern spelling and punctuation.

1   Ed. F. Toennies, 1889, reprinted 1969, Frank Cass, London.—EDS.
2   Page references in the following are to the Cambridge University Press edition by Waller, reprinted 1935.—EDS.
3   Otto v. Gierke, *Johannes Althusius*, third ed., p. 300.
4   "The greatest part of those men who have written aught concerning commonwealths, either suppose, or require us, or beg of us to believe, that man is a creature born fit for society. The Greeks call him *zoon politikon.*"

In the first annotation he says: "Since we see actually a con-stituted society among men, and none living out of it; since we discern all desirous of congress and mutual correspondence: it may seem an amazing kind of stupidity to lay in the very threshold of this doctrine such a stumbling block before the readers, as to deny man to be born fit for society," Hobbes says. The annotation was, as one may infer as probable, called for by the fact that some of his readers had expressed in strong terms their astonishment at this paradox. Hobbes, it appears, was prepared in defense of his theory to make one important concession. It was true, he admitted, that no human being could live in solitude, nor an infant even be-gin to enjoy living without the aid of others, "wherefore I deny not that men, even nature compelling, desire to come together." Political societies, however—and the operative word is "political" —are not a mere matter of getting together but they are alliances, and to establish an alliance, trust and a compact are needed. Chil-dren and uneducated persons, Hobbes goes on, are unable to recognize the nature of these; those who have no experience of the damage that results from the absence of society do not know its usefulness. The ones, who do not understand what society is, can-not enter it; the others, who do not know what it is good for, do not care. "Yet have they, infants as well as those of riper years, a human nature; wherefore man is made fit for society not by na-ture, but by education. Furthermore, although man were born in such a condition as to desire it, it follows not that he therefore were born fit to enter it; for it is one thing to desire, another to be in capacity for what we desire; for even they, who through their pride will not stoop to equal conditions without which there can be no society, do yet desire it."

Critical evaluation. Hobbes has often been praised for the rigorous consistency in his thinking. Indeed the energy with which he knows how to pursue an argument is admirable. But how brittle at certain points those lines of thought are by which he undertook to establish that remarkable political theory of his, I have shown in my early paper of 1880.[5] In the interpretation to which my own

[5]   Notes on the philosophy of Hobbes I–IV, in *Vierteljahrsschrift fuer wissenschaftliche Philosophie*, 1879–80.

studies have led me, the original conception of the theory was as follows.

In the state of nature man is determined by his emotions, he is frightened of others; for various reasons men conflict with each other, and a state of war is the outcome. In the civil state it is the reasonableness of the possessor of political power which compels people to be amenable, and a state of peace is the outcome. A political power can arise out of the state of nature only in this way, that human beings, through the experience of the state of war, arrive at the insight that to end this terrible state they must create that thing called the State: its essential nature being the complete and unconditional possession and exercise of power, whether by a single or a collective person.

This fundamental idea, which ever so often recurs in his writings, is as it were pushed over by the new theory of the human mind, which Hobbes derived from his scientific and mathematical studies, more particularly from the mechanistic physiology he had learned from William Harvey. The gist of this theory is that the human will is exclusively determined by emotions, and that this determination is a necessary one: human will is emotionally egotistic, and cannot but be egotistical. Greed and fear are the dominant motives. This theory leads Hobbes to the conclusion that only out of fear, that is to say mutual fear, can society be produced. Greed will only move man to subdue and to dominate others. Mutual fear, and mutual distrust as its motive power, were also attributed to the state of nature, and therefore belonged to the general state of enmity. That, according to his own principles, it was a paradox to derive from the same source not only sociability but political power cannot have escaped the author of this theory, and it was presumably this contradiction to which some of his readers drew his attention.

In the second annotation to *De Cive* he tried to meet their objection that the effect of mutual fear must be that human beings could not even bear to look at each other face to face. He explains that by fear he means foresight or prudence, which most often leads to the attempt to cover oneself with weapons and other means of defense—"whence it happens that daring to come forth, they know each other's spirits; but then, if they fight, civil society arises from victory, if they agree, from their agreement."

This line of reasoning betrays Hobbes' perplexity. In the text to which this annotation relates, a power that quite obviously refers to the state as a fruit of victory had been clearly distinguished from the society (domination versus society): for domination, men would strive with all their greed if they were not kept in check by fear. We note that the philosopher, who places such a high value on definition, fails here to define what he means by society. Does he mean the same thing when he talks of society as such (in the text) as when he talks of civil society (in the annotation)? And is the latter, or are both, to be thought of as equivalent to the state (*civitas*)? Or, are only the "great and lasting societies" the same as the state?

The circumstantial argument. Just as Hobbes found it necessary to answer the objections about the *zoon politikon*, so it is probable that the passage in the text itself which criticized the Aristotelian concept was designed to meet an objection that had been raised in writing or in conversation, whether an objection against his English treatise (*The Elements*), known only by a few handwritten copies, or raised when he developed in conversation his theorem of the war of all against all. With such an objection he might have dealt in the following way, which would have been in line with the rest of his political theory, namely:

If your understanding of the *zoon politikon* is that it means that man cannot live without his fellowmen, one needs the other for his aid, for company, for intercourse, and for communication, then I agree wholeheartedly. The only reservation I, Hobbes, would have to make is that love and goodwill are only to a small part man's motives; it is far more his selfish motives on which the urge to be sociable and to live in society is based. But the selfish motives—and it is they that are second nature to man—lead far more often to quarrel and conflict, or even to open fighting and to war, than to harmony, obedience, and peace. Moreover, the peaceful relationships, for example, between husband and wife, parents and children, are often torn by antagonism, a domineering attitude, and revolt; in the state of nature there is no guarantee that they may last, none of permanent peace, hence no security against hostile attacks, although a sensible person who does not want to quarrel with himself must long for peace and security. ("Whosoever therefore holds that it had been best to have continued in that state, in which all things were lawful for all men, he contradicts himself." *De Cive* I 13.) This need is not satisfied by contracts, where everyone remains independent of everyone else, and which everyone may renounce whenever it seems to be to his advantage. It is not sufficient that, motivated by mutual fear, men come to hold the view that it is better to abandon the general state of war or to alleviate it by seeking allies by force or persuasion. Nor can one maintain oneself permanently by tyranny, which those who are being tyrannized will always try to escape. This need can be satisfied only by setting up a commonwealth, to whose established authorities, recognized by all as legal, those belonging together ("all") voluntarily and cognizant of its common benefits consider themselves subject. Such a commonwealth, by its very constitution, is a work of art. The civil state, which thereby is created, is an artificial state. Perhaps it can never be achieved in perfection, and it can be achieved only by cultivated people, who by restraint (*disciplina* was the term used in that first annotation) or by education (this is the term used in the English translation of that annotation) have learned to understand what is to their true advantage, and to take thought of the future. ("They therefore who could not agree concerning a present, do agree concerning a future good, which indeed is a work of reason; for things present are obvious to the sense, things to come to our reason only." *De Cive* III 31.)

As is suggested by the quotations I have given here, and as will be noted by the attentive reader, most pieces of this line of thought are really there as fragments, but in the text and the annotations they have not been properly joined. They somehow remain lopsided. Why is this? Because the final piece is missing, that is, the clear and complete distinction of a commonwealth, not just from any society or from sociability at large but as much from the "great and lasting societies," from alliances, from all forms of social life, which are possible also in the state of nature, and actually occur in it, and which as such belong to the state of nature. Again we must ask, Why?

The development of the political theory. In my book-length study of Hobbes I could show how the abstract-rationalist character of the theory was achieved only gradually in the author's thought.[6] While at the early stages he was still concerned with the basis of empirical states of governments, the definitive formation of the theory grew out of the clear insight that his problem was the abstract idea of the rational state, however far the actual so-called states did or did not measure up to the idea. I also proved that this line of thought did not reach its culmination until *Leviathan,* although even in that work there remain traces of the initial aim at a descriptive explanation of states as they are in reality. Nevertheless, it is only in *Leviathan* that the idea of the state became the main theme. In the first work, *The Elements,* it was the idea of law, in the second, *De Cive,* the idea of the citizen that was his theme. I tried to demonstrate that the progress in Hobbes' thinking was closely linked to the emphasis on the state as a person. In *De Cive,* Hobbes moves in that direction, but the theory becomes dominant only in *Leviathan.* It is there that he fully works out the proposition that the essence of "person" consists in representation (that is, of the words and actions of one or a number of persons, or of those of any other being to whom they can be ascribed, whether as something real or fictional). A natural person is the one that represents only himself, while any other person, being fictitious or artificial, represent the purposes and interests of others. In my paper of 1880 I had made it clear that the concept of the state as a work of art occurs as a dominant concept in *Leviathan,* and that it was in this work that Hobbes compared this political theory of his to architectural principles.

The question of whether man is or is not by nature social was in this context irrelevant. There is no more mention of the *zoon politikon,* and the whole discussion about the exclusively egotistical nature of man, with which it is connected, has been dropped.

---

[6]   Op. cit., 3d ed. [1925], p. 244.

True, he repeats: human beings derive no pleasure but a great deal of grief from being in each other's company when there is no power to keep them in awe. But alongside the causes of conflict in human nature—competition, distrust, vanity—he now discovers as many emotions that induce men to peace; they are fear of death, a desire for the things needed for a pleasant life, the hope of achieving these things by industry. The problem he had formerly approached from the outside, that is, of the possibility as well as the historicity of a change from a state of nature or war to the civil state of peace, thus disappears almost completely. The problem has now been internalized. The war of all against all is always latently there wherever competition, distrust, and vanity predominate; but at the same time these motives are being counteracted by other motives, and these will weigh heavier in the balance once the perfect state in keeping with the new doctrine and its rules has been achieved. Until that happens, the situation remains fraught with faults and the ever present danger of relapse. A series of the relevant passages I put together in my monograph[7] bear out this conception.

To appreciate fully this progress in the idea, it is of interest to compare the statements Hobbes makes about the war of all against all in the three consecutive versions of the theory. The emphasis on the internalized principle is perhaps strongest in one of his late writings (1674),[8] where he declared: "Most grateful, all men will agree, they must be to those who first induced them to get together (*consociarent*) and make contracts to the effect that they obey one supreme power for the sake of keeping the peace (*inter se paciscerentur*). But I would owe the next-greatest thanks to those who can persuade them not to violate their undertakings." A certain wavering is, however, discernible in his work between trust in an established supreme power, whatever its origin, on the one hand, and the stronger trust in better insight and in the effects of scientific understanding, on the other hand. Absolute power re-

---

[7]   Op. cit., pp. 244–48, p. 306, with reference to "Notes on the Philosophy of Hobbes," III, op. cit. pp. 428–56.
[8]   *Principia et problemata aliquot geometrica*, Latin Works ed. Molesworth, vol. V, p. 202.

mains decisive, but to be valid it must be based on common consent, as the expression of an enlightented view—today, one might say, of public opinion.

Argument from experience and abstract idea. The idea that the war of all against all does not reflect chiefly, much less exclusively, the position prior to the civil state, but also or even essentially the position within the civil, orderly, peaceful state is being sounded as early as *De Cive*. Not, however, in the text of that work but in the preface to the reader, which Hobbes wrote later. There he sets down, "in the first place for a principle," by experience known to all men: that the dispositions of men are naturally such that, unless they are restrained through fear of some coercive power, every man will distrust and fear the other; therefore, as by natural right he may, so by necessity he will be forced to, make use of the strength he has toward the preservation of himself:

Perhaps, you will object [Hobbes continues] that there are some who deny this; truly so it happens that very many do deny it. But shall I therefore seem to contradict myself because I affirm that the same men confess and deny the same thing? In trust I do not, but they do whose actions disavow what their words approve of. We see all countries, though they be at peace with their neighbors, yet guarding their frontiers with military installations, their towns with walls and gates, and keeping constant watches. To what purpose is all this, if there be no fear of the neighboring power? We see even in well-governed states, where there are laws and punishments appointed for offenders, yet individual men travel not without being armed for defence, nor do they sleep without shutting not only their doors against their fellow citizens, but also their trunks and coffers against those who share their abode or are their servants. Obviously, individual men as well as governments (states) who act in this fashion confess that they mutually distrust and fear each other. But in a controversy they attempt to deny it, which means that out of a desire to contradict others they end up by contradicting themselves.[9]

In a different context, in the middle of the chapter "Of the Natural Condition of Mankind," *Leviathan* (I 13) reproduces this thought. Here the inference, deduced from the passions, is being

[9]   P. 11/12 ed. Lamprecht.—Eds.

confirmed by experience. "Let him therefore consider with himself, when taking a journey, he arms himself, and seeks to go well accompanied; when going to sleep, he locks his doors, when even in his house, he locks his chests; and this when he knows there be laws and public officers, armed, to revenge all injuries that shall be done him: what opinion he has of his fellow subjects, when he rides armed; of his fellow citizens, when he locks his doors; and of his children and servants, when he locks his chests. Does he not there as much accuse mankind by his actions, as I do by my words?" Immediately following this, Hobbes concedes that "there never was such a time, nor condition of war as this; and I believe it was never generally so, over all the world: but there are many places where they live so now." Renewed mention of the "savage people in many places in America" ("except the government of small families, the concord whereof depends on natural lust") is followed by a sentence that is pregnant with conceptual significance; it reads, "Howsoever, it may be perceived what manner of life there would be, where there were no common power to fear, by the manner of life into which men that have formerly lived under a peaceful government usually degenerate during a civil war." The same idea occurs in the 1656 polemic about free will with the Bishop Bramhall, where he says, "There are therefore almost at all times multitudes of lawless men."[10]

Finally, Hobbes refers again as decisive ("though there had never been any time, wherein particular men were in a condition of war one against another" [*Leviathan, ibid.*] "since the creation there never was a time in which mankind was totally without society" [Bramhall polemic]) to the example of the relations between different countries, or, more precisely, "kings and persons of sovereign authority, because of their independency, are in continual jealousies, and in the state and posture of gladiators; having their weapons pointing, and their eyes fixed on one another, that is their forts, garrisons and guns upon the frontiers of their kingdoms; and continual spies upon their neighbors; which is a posture of war." Curious the remark he adds: "But because they uphold

10   *The Questions concerning liberty, necessity and chance*, etc., No. XIV, English Works ed. Molesworth, vol. V, p. 184.

thereby the industry of their subjects, there does not follow from it that misery which accompanies the liberty of particular men."[11]

Hobbes wrote in the years when the Thirty Years' War on the European continent was drawing to its end, and at that time, no less than today, there would seem to have been good reason to describe the misery of nations in analogy to that of individuals in a state of anarchy. In the seventeenth century, however, permanent armed forces were only in their beginnings. On the same plane as the analogy between the situation of individuals and that of countries is the viewpoint of international law as an applied general natural law, resting as it does on a rational concept of equality, with peace as its aim. Thus as early as in the last line of *The Elements*,[12] again in *De Cive* at greater length,[13] and in *Leviathan*.[14]

The old contrast superseded. There are other indications that Hobbes came to recognize his theory for what it was, that is, a strictly hypothetical scheme, or an ideal construct, invented for the comparison with the antistate.

One of his French correspondents acknowledged, under the date of January 4, 1657, the reply he had received to his own draft thesis; he wrote, "I find that you do not quite do justice to the state of nature by the illustration of the soldiers who serve on different sides, and that of the masons who work under different architects."[15] I would explain this as follows. Hobbes wanted to indicate by these illustrations that wherever people are not subject to the same regimen, and do not live under the same constitution, there is in fact something analogous to the state of nature —they do not want any dealings with each other, they remain strangers

---

[11]   *Leviathan* I 13, op. cit., p. 85.

[12]   ["For that which is the law of nature between men and men, before the constitution of the commonwealth, is the law of nations between sovereign and sovereign, after."] *Elements* II 10.10, p. 151, ed. Toennies.

[13]   *De Cive* XIV 4, p. 158.

[14]   *Leviathan* II 30, p. 257.

[15]   From these letters—Hobbes's own letters seem to have been lost, at least, they have as yet not been traced—I made some extracts in 1878 at the Hardwicke hunting lodge in Devonshire where Hobbes died on December 4, 1679. They are kept with some other remains of his in a file "The Hobbes Papers."

to each other, and are potentially opposed to each other. Whether the examples he gave were a happy choice, I would doubt with his French correspondent. It is possible that Hobbes replied once more, and tried to make his meaning clearer. He may in such a letter even have reverted to the question of the *Zoon Politikon*.[16] That he did eventually come up with a different view, as far as the Aristotelian formula is concerned, seems to me cannot be doubted. Such insight was bound to come to him the more he grew conscious of "the state as a work of art"—this, two centuries later, was going to be theme and title of the first part of Jakob Burckhardt's great work on *The Civilization of the Renaissance in Italy*—and it was this very conception to which he was led when he reexamined, in *De Cive*, his own introductory disquisition. Admittedly, the thesis of the ancient Greek philosopher, according to which the *polis* existed *physei*, and man was *physei* a being that was made teleologically for the *polis* (this being the true meaning of the famous sentence), cannot apparently be reconciled with the idea of a work-of-art state. I say "apparently," for the truth of the matter is that the remarks in *Leviathan* I quoted earlier show how Hobbes had indeed widened the conception by combining in his own theory the empirically descriptive study of existing countries as imperfect and faulty edifices with the pure theory of the topic as such and the rules of a consistent political architecture.

The result of this was that he could entertain as a possibility a progressive approximation of the real to the ideal—"Time and industry produce every day new knowledge . . . long after men have begun to constitute commonwealths, imperfect and apt to relapse into disorder, there may principles of reason be found out, by industrious meditation, to make their constitution (excepting by external violence) everlasting."[17] Compare with this the re-

---

16   Of the numerous letters he wrote to France some may quite possibly still be preserved in provincial libraries. I have searched the libraries in Paris, and not without success, see my "Seventeen Letters to Samuel Sorbière" etc. in *Archiv fuer Geschichte der Philosophie*, vol. III, 1898, pp. 58–71 [and the reprint by G. C. Robertson in *Mind*, vol. XV, pp. 440–47].
17   *Leviathan* II, chapter 30, p. 244, which I quoted in full in my monograph, 3d ed., p. 232.

mark that he was "at the point of believing this my labour as useless as the commonwealth of Plato," yet recovered some hope
"that at one time or another this writing of mine may fall into the
hands of a sovereign, who will . . . convert this truth of speculation
into the utility of practice."[18]

In a general sense, Hobbes could have said that the ancient
antithesis of things existing *physei* and of things existing *nomo* or
thesei was not absolutely valid; it was valid, in that the thinking
about things existing *nomo* or *thesei* was a construction, that is, an
abstract concept. But in reality art and the exercise of art belong to
human nature, which by its very capacity for abstract thought distinguishes itself from animal nature.[19] In the political theory itself,
however, this view was not decisively followed up by Hobbes. The
original conception proved too strong, as is particularly evident in
his discussion about social animals (bees and ants), which occurs
in all three versions. Each time Hobbes insisted, apart from other
circumstances that distinguish human beings and counteract their
natural harmony, that in the last analysis the agreement among
those animals was natural but among men "by covenant only,
which is artificial."[20] Had Hobbes at this point added words to
the effect that the artifact based on reason is for man, because he
is capable of reasoning, as natural as is instinctive or emotionally
conditioned social behavior for certain animals, he would have expressed only what fully accords with his whole way of thinking.

More clearly than in the discussion about social animals, this
way of thinking comes to the fore in the last of Hobbes' principal
works, *De Homine* (1658). Here he lists the most important advantages man reaps from being endowed with speech. They are:
first, the ability to count (which is considered at some length);
second, the ability to advise and instruct; and third,

That we can give orders and understand orders, is a benefit of speech,
and a very great one at that. Without this, there would be no society

[18]   Op. cit., II, chapter 31 [p. 268, Cambridge ed.—EDS.].
[19]   "We speak of art as distinguished from nature, but art itself is
natural to man," as Adam Ferguson declared in *An Essay on the History
of Civil Society*, 1767. [ed. Duncan Forbes, Edinburgh 1966, p. 6.—EDS.]
[20]   *Leviathan* II, chapter 17, p. 118.

among men, no peace, and consequently no high culture; but savageness, first, then solitude, and caves for dwelling-places. For although
some animals have got some states (*politiae*) of their own sort, these
are not adequate for the good life; they do not therefore deserve being
considered here, and they are contrived by animals that are defence-
less and have no great needs; man is not among their number, and as
swords and shields, the weapons of man, are superior to those of animals, their horns, teeth and claws, so is man superior to bears, wolves
and snakes. They are not greedy beyond their immediate hunger and
savage only when provoked, but man surpasses them in his greed and
savageness, he is famished even to the point where he strives to still his
future hunger. From which it will be easily understood how much we
owe to speech. By means of speech we socialize and, reaching agreement by means of contract, live securely, happily and in a refined
manner; in other words, we are able to live because we will it so.[21]

But, this line of thought continues, speech is also afflicted by
evil consequences. It is due to speech that man can err more and
worse than other animals. Furthermore, he can lie and arouse enmity in the minds of his fellowmen to the conditions of society and
peace; animal societies are not exposed to this. In addition, man
can repeat words he has not understood, assuming he is saying
something when in fact he says nothing. Finally, he can deceive
himself with words, which again the beast cannot do. "Therefore,
by speech does man become not better, only more powerful."[22]

Individualism. No trace whatever can be found in Hobbes of
an idea which is more appropriate for us today than his view of the
original state of life, or the state of nature hidden beneath civilization: the idea, that is, that the modern, urbanized, *Gesellschaft*-like
civilization, of which he knew only the beginnings, represents a
concealed war of all against all. Yet this is in fact the real substance of his theme, even if in abstract expression and in form of a
model, which can claim to be conceptually as accurate as the statement that our planet is a sphere. "Individualism" has often been
described as the very nature of our age, and hardly ever in such
depth of historical insight as in Burckhardt's *Civilization of the
Renaissance in Italy*. It is this individualism that as an eternal truth

21   *De Homine* X 3, Latin Works ed. Molesworth, vol. II, p. 91.
22   Ibid.

was made the foundation of Hobbes' system of political philosophy. The generally observable conflict among individuals is indeed the consequence of their unconditional self-affirmation. Our more recent times, with their unfettered economic competition, their class struggles, their contests between political parties, and their civil wars, have more and more revealed that Medusa's head (to borrow an expression of Marx)[23] that hides itself under the veil of the presumably highest achievements of civilization, such as the triumphant progress of technology, of worldwide communications, and of science.

[23]   Preface to the first edition of *Das Kapital.*

The Concept of Gemeinschaft

For a long time it has been accepted as an achievement of German scientific endeavor that it supplemented the concept of the state, which from of old had occupied the central place in the philosophy of law, by that of society. The essential merit for this is ascribed to Hegel, who, in his lectures on *The Philosophy of Right*, places "civil society" as the second link—the antithesis—between the family and the state, making these three combined phenomena, which reach consummation, of course, in the third, the realization of right (or law) as the moral order (*Sittlichkeit*). In attaching to society the adjective "civil," he takes up an expression which had become current in the French and English literature of the eighteenth century—for instance, through Ferguson's *Essay on the History of Civil Society* (1767)—although no attempt had yet been made to render this expression as a concept. Hegel had an eminent successor in Lorenz Stein, who (for the first time in 1849) expounded "the concept of society and the principles of its transformation" as an opening chapter to the *History of the Social Movement in France since 1789*. He wanted to show in this work that the constitution and administration of a state are subject to the static elements and dynamic movements of the social order. The economic order, he said, becomes, by means of the division of labor, a social order, comprising man and his activities; and the social order, in turn, through the family, becomes a lasting order of the generations. Within the social order, moreover, the community of men is the organic unity of their lives; "and this organic unity of human life is human society." Stein goes on to argue that the content of the life of the human "community" (*Gemeinschaft*) must be a continuous struggle between state and society, the state, being, to him, the "community" of men asserting itself, as if it were a personality, in will and action. The principle of the state rests with its task of developing

---

Translated from "Der Begriff der Gemeinschaft," *Soziologische Studien und Kritiken* 2 (1925): 266–76; the latter part of this paper, about one fourth of the whole, has been omitted.

itself and, for the sake of that self-development, to strive with its highest power for the progress, wealth, vigor, and intelligence of all individuals encompassed by it. The principle of society, on the other hand, is interest, hence the subjection of individuals by other individuals, that is, the fulfillment of the individual by means of the dependence from it of the other individual.

This theory, which Stein applied and unfolded ingeniously, won its most important follower in Rudolf Gneist, whose influence helped to shape the constitutional and administrative law of Prussia and of the new German Reich. In his treatise on the *Rechtsstaat*, Gneist sets out by acknowledging that the contemporary world, with its deep antagonisms, can be understood only on the ground of *Gesellschaft*. "Science, too," he says, "is compelled to acknowledge that the abstract 'I' from which the older natural law constructed the state is not a part of the real world; that in reality every people is divided and articulated according to the possession and acquisition of the external and spiritual goods which mankind is ordained to acquire and enjoy—an articulation which I comprise, in this treatise, in the concept of "society" (*Gesellschaft*)." And, in a note, Gneist makes reference to "Stein's masterly explication," which, he adds, was of decisive importance for his own treatment of English constitutional history.

If the concepts "state" and "society" are placed side by side, the first observation to which the juxtaposition gives rise is that while the latter term merely denotes a collectivity of men interrelated in manifold ways, the term state, whatever its other connotations, indicates at any rate an association—a union or, as is customary to say nowadays, an organization—to which so and so many persons belong who, to begin with, live next to each other in a "state territory." Against the theory of modern natural law according to which the state proceeded, like another association (*"Sozietaet"*), from the will of the individuals, the historical school of jurisprudence had revolted by declaring that the state was something that had grown, something organic, something original in its core, and not at all brought into existence by contract. This polemic against the natural law theory resulted from a misunderstanding of that doctrine and, at the same time, from a conservative (or restorative) intention to impede the activity of the state that arose from the French Revolution as well as from the princely absolutism that had preceded it and whose avocation and fitness for legislation and codification were denied by the outstanding founder of the historical school (Savigny).

Nevertheless, it must be granted and understood that another construction of the state, as well as of other associations, is possible than that which represents it as a means for the common ends of a great many individual persons; even if it were thought of as a means, it must not necessarily be thought of as an isolated, mechanical means, but may also be an end, so indissolubly intertwined with the common ends of a multitude of individuals that it in fact expresses them by and in itself. For an association may, by its "members," not only be called but also conceived of as a "corporation," essentially independent from the members, as parts, and—while its component parts change, and through that very change—maintaining itself as a living entity or organism. And just as in the case of an association, a mere relationship of two or more men will appear one way if these men are thought of as essentially strange to each other but meeting in their wishes and interests and entering into an exchange relationship for mutual advantage—and another way if it is thought that there is something that they have in common to begin with from which mutual services result as a consequence. The thing they have in common may be, for instance, common descent; but also a common end such as the founding of a common household, that is, if the latter is thought of not as an object of wishes that are incidentally coinciding but as a common incumbency, a duty, and a necessity. In the same manner, all social values which the individual shares either by unreservedly feeling and thinking them as belonging to him or by a mere relationship of high valuation may be thought of in two different ways: either as objective or, in the perfect case, sacred values which exist and persist independently from the evaluating participant although the participant shares in their enjoyment as a companion (*Genosse*); or as caused by the individuals who severally recognize and posit the value. In the first case, the common value is to be conceived of as an indivisible totality or at least one which, if divided, flows back again into one whole. In the second case, the common value is to be conceived of as composed of the contributions of individuals, always remaining divisible, a mere quantity of means intended for a more or less limited end.

I thought it necessary to state that all social relationships, social values, and social unions and associations, insofar as they exist for their subjects—the social men—are created, posited, or instituted by the will of the latter, and that it is this psychological conditioning which constitutes their essence because, in this manner, they are seen, as it were, from within. This stands in contrast to Stein's definition of the concept of society, or *Gesellschaft*, ("the organic labor in human life"), which remains stuck to the outside of things. Moreover, community, or *Gemeinschaft*, with Stein, is merely an expression meaning that "the whole exists for the sake of the parts." Consequently, he calls society (*Gesellschaft*) and the state "the two great elements of *Gemeinschaft*." (*System der Staatswissenschaft*, vol. 2.)

In contradistinction to this usage, the foremost principle for the subdivision of the social entities must be found in the differing quality of the human will which is contained in them and, indeed, is the maxim of their existence. This becomes more evident if the noun "will," which is a *perfectum*, is replaced by the verb "to affirm," which is in the present mode, so that we may speak of the affirmation of social relationships, social values, and social associations. The sharpest contrast, then, arises if affirmation of a social entity for its own sake is distinguished from an affirmation of such an entity because of an end, or purpose, which is extraneous to it. I call a will of the first kind *essential will*, and a will of the second kind *arbitrary will*. Evidently, this view differs strongly from a theory which is sometimes encountered and which distinguishes "involuntary" from willed or voluntary unions, associations, and so on, and as the former regards, by a definition which is merely external, those which did not originate from a specific decision of the individuals concerned and therefore can be said to be "without will," as, for instance, the family into which one is born. In fact, however, it may be supposed to be the normal case that a man affirms his family with all his heart, so that he posits it by his

essential will, precisely as he posits by his arbitrary will a commercial company, which has the limited purpose of maintaining
the value of an investment and deriving the highest possible profit
from it.

Further, this view in no way coincides with that which con-
ceives of "spontaneous organizations" as originating from feeling
and instinct. In the first place, I do not emphasize the genetic aspect, but a lasting inner relationship. For instance, a marriage—
to consider a very individual relationship—may be entered into
very enthusiastically, for its own sake, and yet after a short time
be maintained and affirmed by both spouses simply with a view to
"what people say," for the sake of social respectability, as a means
to maintain one's position and the position of one's children in
society: in other words, as a *marriage de convenance*. Second, my
synthetic concepts of essential will and arbitrary will do not correspond to the distinction of instinctual and volitional actions, as
these terms are used by Wundt and others. Essential will definitely
comprises what psychologists would call volitional actions inasfar
as they affirm means and ends as an organic whole, that is, as a
belonging together. The concept of arbitrary will arises, as it
were, only when and to the extent that means and ends become
separated (become alienated from each other), to the point even
of becoming outright antagonistic to each other. A perfect arbitrary
will affirms a relationship, even in spite of a definite aversion to it
—that is, exclusively for the sake of the desired end. For instance,
a hike in the mountains, the aim of which is to reach a high sum-
mit, I will affirm and welcome as a whole thing, despite great difficulties and labors. But I will consent to a train trip from Eutin to
Berlin—especially under the conditions obtaining in 1919—only
for the sake of its aim and end. I will make this decision reluc-
tantly insofar as I am thinking of the trip itself, which is envisaged
merely as the unavoidable means for reaching my goal. As a rule,
some of the pleasurable connotations of the end will be communi-
cated to the means, just as the displeasure caused by the actor to
others reflects back to the actor himself; but the more cold reasoning strives to reach the end, seeking it unconditionally, the more
will the reasoning human being become indifferent against unin-

tended consequences and incidental phenomena connected with its pursuit—both in concrete reality and in anticipatory thought; he will become indifferent to his own immediate displeasure and even more so to the displeasure caused to others, and to the compassion which may stir in him. All these relationships are conceived of still more generally, if the more general concepts of affirmation and negation are applied. For precisely as the person motivated by arbitrary will disregards inner displeasures, so will he disregard other forms of inner negation; for instance, he will use words which he cannot truly affirm or which he even knowingly negates; in other words, he will deliberately tell an untruth calculated to deceive others.

On the other hand, volitional acts, including words, remain within the meaning of the concept of essential will, if these words are spoken in full conviction, even though they may at the same time be used with a view to gaining some end. Likewise, a relationship which is affirmed through love or affection, or because it has become dear through custom and habit or in the line of duty, remains within the concept of *Gemeinschaft* (community) even though it may at the same time be thought of and appreciated in full recognition of its usefulness to me, the affirmer.

The concept of community in this subjective sense must be strictly distinguished from the concept, or, rather, notion, which common speech intends in combinations such as folk or ethnic community, community of speech, community of work (*Volksgemeinschaft, Sprachgemeinschaft, Werkgemeinschaft*) and so forth. Here, reference is only to the objective fact of a unity based on common traits and activities and other external phenomena. Stein took his misconception of community from this common usage. To be sure, bridges exist between this external (objective) and the internal, or intimate, (subjective) concept of community which I am using and which, likewise, has affinity to common usage. All forms of external community among men comprise the possibility, even the probability, of an internal, or intimate, community (communion), and may thus be conceived of as a potential *Gemeinschaft* of those united in it. Thus, the more language rises into consciousness as an element constituting a bond of minds and as a value which is held in common, the more will a linguistic community, instead of being a mere external fact, become a significant and unifying relationship. The same is true of the community of descent, which is closely akin to, though not fully identical with, the community of language; true, that is, of the folk community or the nation. In this sense, with which I agree, it was said that on August 4, 1914, the German people became a community. It is somewhat different with a religious community, which, to be sure, can be considered merely in its external shape or form but which, essentially at least, intends and ought to be an intimate community or communion. For it is its very essence that men who pray to, and conceive of, the same God feel bound to each other and that they wish to be bound to each other by a common consciousness. This is especially so if they conceive of themselves as members of a mystical body, the Church, and still more so if they believe that they partake of and receive into themselves the divine head of the Church by participating in a "communion," whereby they enter into a suprasensual-sensual bond with that divine head, and hence with each other.

I proposed three kinds of internal, or intimate, community, distinguished by the familiar terms kinship, neighborhood, friendship. The first two of these frequently and simultaneously designate merely external facts or things, which, indeed, they often are.[24] One can say that the idea of community (*Gemeinschaft*) attains fulfillment in friendship, in contrast to the counterconcept of hostility, even though it should be noted that no type of inner community excludes hostile feelings and conduct of those associated in it as factual phenomenon. A relationship, for instance, a marriage, may in the consciousness of those associated in it exist as an essential community and yet often be disturbed by such feelings or conduct. To be sure, they corrode the community and may dissolve it internally, although it may continue to exist externally, even though confirmed by the will and consent of those associated in it. It has then become a societal (*Gesellschaft*-like) relationship in the sense mentioned above. In order to supplement what we

---

[24]   Also, friendship, so called, in the superficial sense of acquaintance, would have to be considered as a predominantly external relationship.— EDS.

have said of communal relationships with names of true comunal unions, I am adding here the terms family, local community (*Gemeinde*), and fellowship (*Genossenschaft*).

Parallel with these divisions and permeating them there is, finally, a distinction by which I discern, as both foundation and expression of *Gemeinschaft*, being together (*Zusammenwesen*), living together (*Zusammenwohnen*), and working, or acting, together (*Zusammenwirken*). If, in contrast to linguistic usage, being (*Wesen*) is here used as a verb, this is done in order to express that through the combination with the term together what is called being becomes an activity, a psychological process. Being together means belonging together raised to consciousness, living together means the affirmation of spatial proximity as precondition of manifold interactions, and working together means these interactions themselves, as emanating from a common spirit and an essential will. Being together, so to speak, is the vegetative heart and soul of *Gemeinschaft*—the very existence of *Gemeinschaft* rests in the consciousness of belonging together and the affirmation of the condition of mutual dependence which is posed by that affirmation. Living together may be called the animal soul of *Gemeinschaft*; for it is the condition of its active life, of a shared feeling of pleasure and pain, of a shared enjoyment of the commonly possessed goods, by which one is surrounded, and by the cooperation in teamwork as well as in divided labor. Working together may be conceived of as the rational or human soul of *Gemeinschaft*. It is a higher, more conscious cooperation in the unity of spirit and purpose, including, therefore, a striving for common or shared ideals, as invisible goods that are knowable only to thought. Regarding being together it is descent (blood), regarding living together it is soil (land), regarding working together it is occupation (*Beruf*) that is the substance, as it were, by which the wills of men, which otherwise are far apart from and even antagonistic to each other, are essentially united.

With respect to being together, the deepest contrast among human beings, especially with respect to its psychological consequences, is the biological difference of sex; as a consequence, men and women always part with each other while at the same time they are attracted to each other; the principle of what is eternally female (*das Ewig-Weibliche*),[25] or the principle of motherliness, is the root of all being together. Men depart more readily and farther from the natural foundation of essential will and *Gemeinschaft*. Correspondingly, women persist more readily in the forms of understanding, custom, and faith, which are the simplest forms of communal will; men find it easier to pass on to those of contract, statute, doctrine as the simple forms of societal will. As men and women live together, so is the same kind of interdependence required for all forms of communal will. This last observation also applies to the discussion that follows.

The deepest contrast with respect to living together is that indicated by the concepts of country and city. This contrast is akin to, and of a similar kind as, the aforementioned one. The countryside, not unlike women, abides in the forms of understanding, custom, and faith, while the city develops the forms of contract, statute, and doctrine. But the city remains surrounded by and, in a way, dependent upon the country, as the male does upon the female. The city emancipates itself from the countryside the more pronouncedly the more it becomes a metropolis (*Grosstadt*).

Again, a similar deep contrast is discernible with regard to working together. This is most plainly indicated by the traits of poverty and wealth. In the present context, however, I want to relate it particularly to the spiritual-moral area, in which it appears as the contrast of the uneducated mass of the common people and their educated rulers. The common people (to use this term for brevity) remain more faithful to understanding, custom, and faith, and are caught in or bound to these forms; those that are educated are more dependent upon contract, statute, doctrine, and these forms, in turn, require education as a necessary condition more than the former do. But also the relation of the essential dependence of the educated strata upon the common people resembles the dependence of city upon country and of men upon women.

As the sexes depend upon living together in a nexus of kin relations, through marriage and the family, so stand country and city, the mass of the people and the ruling class, in mutual de-

25   The expression is taken from the last act of Goethe's *Faust*.—EDS.

pendence upon each other. Especially, country and city need to live in peaceable neighborliness; the mass of the people and the ruling class, in addition, must live in a kind of friendship and companionship of mutual trust. Intensive forms of communal living together resemble a companionship in a common struggle.

In all these relationships, there are many other important differentiations besides those mentioned, partly paralleling them, partly mingling with them.

In being together, there is not only the contrast of the sexes but also, in a less pronounced way, that of the ages. In this respect there is a certain duality of young and old, especially regarding children, or sexually immature, and adults, or sexually mature persons.

In living together, there is the differentiation not only of city and country but already of the more densely populated countryside and a widely dispersed population; consequently, of the rural folks of the plains from that of the mountains, of that of the fertile marshes (*Marschen*) from that of the high and dry land and the heath (*Geest* and *Heide*).[26] Likewise, the big city stands in contrast to the small country town, and so does the big city, or metropolis, to country and small towns taken together; and even more so contrasts the capital city to the provincial towns and cities, and the cosmopolitan megalopolis to all other towns and cities. Furthermore, whole regions and areas differ in the same respect, and so do, under the influence of different geographic and cultural conditions, entire ethnic groups. All these differences partly are parallel to and partly overlap the differences between country and city.

In working together, there is—comparable to the differentiation between the mass of the people and the ruling class—the differentiation of a variety of occupational groupings within the people and of estates (*Staende*) within the ruling stratum. As to the people, we have the distinction of menial laborers and traders, and within the laboring classes there is the distinction of agricultural and industrial labor (the crafts). As to the ruling stratum, there are

[26]   These terms refer to ecological regions in Schleswig-Holstein.— EDS.

different dominant estates, especially the ecclesiastic and the secular estate. Within the secular estate, finally, there is an older substratum, essentially tied to landed estates, and a younger substratum, essentially powerful through the disposition over capital.

II. Elaboration of Concepts

EDITORS' NOTE. *Between the years 1899 and 1924 Toennies clarified the concepts which he had first formulated in* Gemeinschaft und Gesellschaft. *The earliest of these pieces,* Prelude to Sociology, *is nearest in time and content to the book that made its author famous. The second, a paper read before a gathering of the Gehe Foundation in 1907, presents the most mature formulation of Toennies' basic ideas. The earlier St. Louis Exposition paper of 1904,* The Present Problems of Social Structure, *bears a certain resemblance to it, yet differs because it was written in response to a specific assignment. Inasmuch as the paper addresses itself to an American audience, Toennies is intent to draw attention to the then prevailing differences between Germany and the English-speaking countries with regard to the theoretical approach to social studies; his references to Spencer and Morgan are particularly noteworthy.*

Part II concludes with the paper The Divisions of Sociology *(the Naples paper) of 1924. This paper foreshadows the major work that Toennies published in his later years,* Introduction to Sociology *(1931).*

5

A PRELUDE TO SOCIOLOGY

THE UNITY of a number of human beings, like every unity, can be conceived in two ways. Either it exists prior to the multiplicity of individualities which is derived from it, or the multiplicity is earlier and unity, or union, is its creation. In observable nature, the first case marks the essence of an organism, the second denotes the inorganic aggregate as well as the mechanical artifact. In the first case, unity is a reality, it is the thing in and of itself; in the second case, unity is of an ideal nature, that is, conditioned by human thought; and thought, in turn, whether on the basis of sensual perception or not, arrives at the image and finally at the concept of the totality which we call unity. Inasmuch as, moreover, totality, or a whole, is composed of its parts, a unity can, and perhaps must, be thought of as the creation of the parts; this remains true even in the event that the composition of the parts has been forced ino being by human will. The cooperation of the parts in the same direction and in uniform motion in the latter case is the purpose and in the former, at least, the consequence of the composition of the whole. This direction or motion, then, already something immaterial, is the common element, it is part and parcel of objective reality, and basic for thought.

The same contrast is repeated when unities, or totalities, are considered which as such are in no way initially given for the per-

Translated from "Zur Einleitung in die Soziologie," *Soziologische Studien und Kritiken* 1 (1925): 65–74; the last paragraph has been omitted, and the notes have been abridged.

ception of the senses (because they are nothing but a multiplicity of similar objects) and therefore require a particular energy of thought to be recognized and thereby to gain a quasi-objective existence. Such is the nature of the general (*universale*), which relates to particular and individual things as a whole does to its parts. It is in this sphere that the famous controversy between realism and nominalism took place, the complete disappearance of which (as a result of the total victory of nominalism) is in the highest degree characteristic of the scientific, and especially the mathematical-physical or mechanical orientation of all modern philosophy. Yet, the truth of realism deserves to be restored. To be sure, it would seem that this truth has lost its last refuge on account of the critique of the concept of species in the theory of evolution, but actually it receives new life from a deeper biological view: for insight into the origin of the species is no detriment to its existence, as it is not detrimental to that of any higher or local group; and in its growth and its acquisition of new abiltiies and loss of those that are no more serviceable, as well as in its progressive differentiation, each species shows that it is alive and active; no less than any individual organism that maintains its essence despite changing parts and by means of the change of its parts.

This treatise pursues the same cardinal antinomy in different, although already indicated, areas. The social unity of men can be understood only psychologically. As a material thing, it must be conceived of in analogy to the individual will, which, however, can borrow its own substantial essence only from the analogy to a material object. On the other hand, even the enduring form of the organic body is something substantial which is accessible only to thought and belongs to psychic as well as physical reality.

At any rate, the social will, or body, is a whole whose parts are human individuals, that is, beings endowed with reason. But this whole, too, either exists prior to the parts or is composed of them. All forms of one kind I call *Gemeinschaft*, all those of the other kind *Gesellschaft*. The germinal forms of *Gemeinschaft* are motherly love, sexual love, brotherly and sisterly love. The elementary fact of *Gesellschaft* is the act of exchange, which presents itself in its purest form if it is thought of as performed by individuals who are alien to each other, have nothing in common with each other, and confront each other in an essentially antagonistic and even hostile manner. Both kinds of unions are universal, and both in a twofold sense. Concerning *Gemeinschaft:* (A) by means of the unity of the species, all men are "brothers" and united through a common ancestor (Adam). However, this idea gains real importance only as restricted to certain peoples or groups of peoples and in connection with religious ideas; (B) the real and most intimate communal relationships are secured as general and necessary by the nature of man. Concerning *Gesellschaft:* (a) as anybody can be anybody's enemy, so can anybody trade with any-body and enter into a contract with him; (b) for this reason an association which, developing from this principle, negates hostility must finally embrace and have as its subjects all men. It is evident that the ideas (A) and (b) converge, while those of (B) and (a) repel each other.

The conceptual constructions are entirely separate and mutually independent. The theory of *Gemeinschaft* is, in the main, a genetic classification of its forms, of which in an ascending series the types of household, village, and town are most noteworthy. The scientific value of this classification is not diminished by the fact that it has been the basis of the social-philosophical discussions of the sages of ancient Greece while it has been neglected in recent times. Indeed, however intricate or confused the political forms of life may be, the above mentioned social, chiefly economic, units are everywhere clearly discernible. They are natural units, or living organisms in a very specific sense, which will be indicated presently. Their becoming and their decline are the real content of cultural history.

The theory of *Gesellschaft*, on the other hand, is purely a matter of thought (*ein reines Gedankending*), a conceptual construction, connected exclusively with the fact and the necessity of existence upon this earth. But as this concept strives toward realization, it finds itself limited by historical conditions. Its first enactment is in the city, dominated, as it is, by the exchange of merchandise whose subjects are free individuals; separated from the material matrix of communal life and thought, they pursue their own ends.

Then follow associations of cities, and of cities and regions, finally enlarged in ever widening circles to *territories*. The process of *Gesellschaft*, entailed in the principle of exchange, primarily denotes the predominance of men who conduct exchange for its own sake and on the basis of their particular skill; that is, the predominance of the commercial class, whose power consists in money as a generalized means of purchase. Further, labor itself—as industry—becomes a branch of commerce, which in industry can most purely free its basic concept, the self-utilization of money, from all accidental conditions (purchase of labor, incorporation of labor in commodities, sale of commodities according to their value). Here we are confronted by the "social question," that is, a condition which demands the resolution of an enigmatic contradiction. In *Gesellschaft*, all individuals are equal insofar as they are capable of engaging in exchange and entering into contracts: that is its concept. The trading, lending, enterprising individuals, as capitalists, are the masters and active subjects of *Gesellschaft*, using the working "hands" as their tools. This is the reality of *Gesellschaft*, inasfar as it develops in the direction indicated; the question as to whether, to what extent, where, and when *Gesellschaft*, and especially this specific condition in *Gesellschaft*, actually exists, must be left to a more specific investigation and analysis.

The content and intent of this theorem can be understood in its entirety only by means of its historical and polemic relations and references. In the book *Gemeinschaft und Gesellschaft* (1887) these relations and references had to be assumed as being present in the reader's mind, so that the book's doctrinal character could be preserved. But there is some reason to suspect that among those who found it worth reading only few actually were sufficiently conversant with the present as well as the past state of doctrines in the philosophy of law and society to be able to notice what was new and contrasting in it. The author therefore believes that he should indicate these points more explicitly than he has done in the preface to *Gemeinschaft und Gesellschaft*.

More recent authors, in their dependence on Hegel, under whose influence all the springs of tradition had been buried, considered it a miraculous achievement on their part to have established the concept of society beside that of the state. Actually this concept of society is nothing but a new version of the old concept of the state of nature (*status naturalis*), which always had been thought of as persisting underneath the political state. The term civil society, too, was not at all unfamiliar in the three principal European countries during the last quarter of the eighteenth century; it was well known that it was civil society that had rebelled against the state in the great revolution and attempted to create a new state. Both the name and the thing subsequently passed to the socialists as heirs of the revolution. To them we owe a combination of the otherwise separate arguments of natural law and political economy, along with an improved historical understanding which is gaining more and more adherents everywhere. The efforts of Lorenz von Stein, which have decisively influenced thinking in the political and social sciences (*Staatswissenschaften*) in Germany, ought to be evaluated in the same sense. However, Stein's theory is best understood as a renewal and basically correct interpretation of the blunt principles of Thomas Hobbes. To wit: Society (*Gesellschaft*), or mankind in its natural state, is characterized by cleavage and hostility; it is the purpose of the state to introduce peace and order in society as well as to restore against the lack of freedom (of the person) and the inequality (of property) which result from the intrinsic movement of society, the ideally conceived equality and liberty. That every empirical state is shaped by society and its social classes, that it emanates from them, and that even that kind of society which is contradictory to the principle of the state uses, and necessarily must use, the state as its instrument —these are conclusions in which (so far as Stein is concerned) the moral postulate of a reform of society comes to terms with the insight into the actual conditions of the present age.

On the other hand, in spite of the fact that his concepts point in all directions, Stein lacks the simple basic schemata and constructions that are required in the theory of law. For it is evident that society and the state fall under the comprehensive concept of an organized group and must be understood according to the general or particular ends which they pursue. The main error, however, rests with the consideration that society and the state are treated as *empirical facts*, supposed to be uniformly present throughout the entire range of our historical knowledge. From the empirical stand-point one can rightly rebel against these concepts, as was done in earnest by the historical school and the theories underlying the politics of the Restoration period. Both influences remain power-ful today. Society, whether taken in its proper sense or in a re-stricted sense encompassing only free and propertied persons, pre-sumably indicates a multitude of individuals, dispersed over an area of some size, engaged in peaceful intercourse, and enforcing the observation of certain rules. Experience simply says: there is no such society. We observe that people are united in households, villages, and towns, in guilds and religious congregations, in coun-tries and empires, ordered by age and sex, and either by achieved or acquired status or occupation; we do not see the mechanical unity which a universal association, wherein all differences between indi-viduals are abolished, would present. What we do see is an inter-connected arrangement of organic units whose origin in an ultimate unit, like a people or ethnic (racial) group, does not need to be clearly and concretely recognizable as long as that origin remains alive as a postulate of reason. Analogously, one can argue against the corresponding definition of the state, although here the *name* in its generalized meaning is maintained. To be sure, the opposition to the rational concept of the state is implicit in the attempts to ex-plain the essence of the state as an organism and consequently in the fervent criticism which supposedly has put the contract theory out of commission; yet the contract theory is naturally appropriate to the reality which we may call the modern state, that is, a struc-ture of thoroughgoing artificiality and marked by a high degree of scientific consciousness.

It is therefore with good reason that the seemingly victorious organic theory of the state recently has been attacked again and that attempts have been made to overthrow it on the grounds that it is useless for the purposes of the jurist. That it doubtless is, not in every sense, but surely in the individualistic sense which is fun-damental to all scientific jurisprudence. For the individualistic point of view, the state must be conceived of as a *person* that exists only in thought or fiction and must be construed in analogy to the *individual* persons whom we know empirically. In Roman jurisprudence, to be sure, there was no thought of a construction of the *res publica*. This is explainable from historical causes. For there was still alive the idea of the urban commonwealth (which, indeed, survived far into the period of the Holy Roman Empire); this commonwealth, in the sum total of its families and through the protection of its gods, appeared as a living, even as an eternal, entity. In contrast, the states and governmental structures of the modern age, although to a moderate extent first developed in free cities and frequently modeled after the example of the Roman empire, arose chiefly from the power of princes, primarily of the Italian city tyrants. This power was absolute, arbitrarily legislating, law destroying and law giving, and elevated high above all subjected wills, customs, and convictions. The important theories of the state of the seventeenth and eighteenth centuries, on the one hand, have arisen from the intention to justify this power; neither as personal power in private law nor as divine power in the Church, which (because it would have meant that the state was conditioned by the Church) would have neutralized the absoluteness of state power, but as general and necessary power in public law; and, on the other hand, from the will to condition and to limit the power of the state.

Certainly, even here the state always remains specifically different from all private associations. It is the *only* person in public law—a confederate state therefore being anomalous—because this quality must be derived from the will and the rights of private persons which exist only *once;* one must think of the general will to defend oneself and to use force to this end and of the monopoly of using force legitimately, which is the essential characteristic of the state. Now, inasfar as it is the simple idea of society (*Gesellschaft*) that it should make possible peaceful intercourse among men, the state is nothing but society itself, setting itself up as a single fictitious person over against the natural, individual persons.

At first glance, my theory appears as a combination of the conflicting organic and mechanical, or historical and rational, theories. But my initial intention was merely to affirm both of these as *possible:* and, indeed, they prove their possibility by their existence. None of these theories is new, but my way of relating and explicating them is new because I juxtapose them without meaning to say that one of them is false and staking an exclusive claim to be right for the other.[1] Does this mean that each is correct in its own way, that each of them contains a fraction of the truth, while the whole truth would have to be sought for in a higher mediating view? I expressed myself otherwise in the preface to the first edition of *G. & G.* where I speak of the doctrine of natural law and the individualistically conceived political economy as the separate disciplines which together express empirically the construct of *Gesellschaft:* "The present theory attempts to absorb these theories and to keep them in a state of dependence." This implies that the "organic" view is the original and comprehensive and, to that extent, the correct theory. Indeed, that is my opinion; consider that I have said that "the strength of *Gemeinschaft* persists, although with diminishing vigor, even in the period of *Gesellschaft* and remains the reality of social life" (p. 252; Loomis, p. 232). The concept of *Gesellschaft*, then, signifies the normal and regular process of decline of all forms of *Gemeinschaft.* This is its truth, and the term *Gesellschaft* is indispensable for the expression of that truth. For this reason it would have to be coined if it had not been formed previously, even if this formation occurred without the awareness of its necessity and real significance. In his treatment of the process of *Gesellschaft*, the author had *modern* society in mind; appropriately he took advantage of the exposure of its "economic law of development" by Karl Marx, as those familiar with the subject will readily recognize and as is expressly noted in the preface to the first edition of *G. & G.*[2]

---

[1]   It is the weakness of the historical school, both in the philosophy of law and in economics, to have arrived at neither a psychological derivation of its social concepts nor a sociological foundation of its psychological concepts. Wherever it attempted to do this, it relapsed into theological or mythological obfuscation.

[2]   I am saying this with some pride because to acknowledge or even to stress Marx's importance for theoretical sociology was quite unheard of in 1887. Accordingly, a reviewer (Albert Schaeffle—Eds.) in the *Zeitschrift fuer die gesamte Staatswissenschaft* (Tuebingen, 1892, p. 559) noted in my book " a not so very weak ingredient of Marxomania." The

It further follows from my presentation that the "organic" the-ory will receive its own proper delimitation only if it is understood psychologically. A quasi-organic character can be imparted to a union of men only by the sensation, emotion, and will of those associated with it: by means of this foundation my theorem is clearly set off from other current "organic" doctrines which do not perceive that by their biological analogies they confine themselves to biology, albeit an expanded one, thus missing the specific char-acteristics of sociological facts. However, the lasting importance and the general scientific value of the position of natural law lie in its opposition to all supernatural explanations and its recognition of the own thought and will of men as the *ratio essendi* of the social structures (*Gebilde*) within which they are moving; natural law fails, however, in that it presents *rational will*, which sharply separates means and ends, as the *only* type of human will, hence comprehends all social relations but as means to individual ends that coincide merely accidentally.

This is precisely why I thought it necessary to draft a theory of the human will, complementary and parallel to social theory. I define as essential will that which corresponds to the concept of *Gemeinschaft* and is basic and essential to it, while by arbitrary will I mean that which corresponds to the concept of *Gesellschaft* and is essential to it, that is, basic to its ideally conceived reality (*ideelle Wirklichkeit*). I conceive of both types as referring to *thinking man* and consequently I call thought the decisive trait of human will generally. But while essential will is will involving thought, arbitrary will is will existing as thought only. The char-acteristic common to them is a thinking (conscious) affirmation

---

observation is not so much denunciatory as superficial. On the other hand, a much earlier review by G. Schmoller (*Jahrbuch*, 1888, pp. 727 ff.) says simply and correctly: "Resonances of Marx characterize these discus-sions" (about the theory of society). But even Schmoller's fair review does not perceive the relation of my theory to the very real and particular problems which are ever-present in the history of thought. I agree with Schmoller entirely, however, when he says that "only those readers will be able to appreciate the book fully who are familiar with the philosoph-ical, historical and socio-political literature on which it is based."

or negation of the object—that is, of a material object or an activity. Affirmation and negation of an object are always reducible to affirmation and negation of an activity. Affirmation is the will to preserve (*conservandi*) the object or to conquer, posit, or possess it—and therefore also the will to create or bring about, to form, or to make it; negation, then, is the will to destroy or remove the object, to dissolve it or to deprive it of its essential properties.

Thinking itself is an activity, involving either affirmation or negation, combination or separation, union or disunion. The thinking affirmation or negation of one object is affirmation or negation with reference to another object, meaning that the objects are brought into relationship to each other; the ideas (thought images, or representations) of the objects are associated with each other. The association of ideas is a likeness of the association of men. It is most significant and important for us as the association of means and ends. The end is what is properly and ultimately wanted. With the idea of the end is that of the means necessarily connected. The question then is: do means and end include or do they exclude each other? If they include each other, they belong to an essential unity, to a whole which is prior to the parts and which dissolves into these by a process of spontaneous differentation. Such an essential unity is found in every creative idea and what is akin to it.

In that case the end is the fulfillment; the means leading to it are the object itself in the stage of development. Product and action condition and include each other. The activities are affirmed because the product is affirmed, and vice versa; the joy of affirmation, and hence the willing, is directed toward the *whole*. The most perfect realization of this idea is found in artistic activity. On the other hand, if the ideas of end and means exclude or negate each other, a unity must be constructed out of them. This is most distinctly the case whenever the end is an event that is not in my power but the means an event that is in my power. In that case, means and end confront each other as if they were strangers and of a different kind; and inasmuch as the one event is a movement which meets an impediment in the movement or position of the other, so that they obstruct each other, it can be said that their confrontation is essentially hostile. Their interaction consists in mutual mechanical coercion; to desire the end becomes the cause of the willing of the means—which is supposed not to be wanted spontaneously—so that the willing of the means becomes the cause that achieves the end. In the first case, the thought-of (ideal) event B is the cause of the real event A; in the second case, the real event A is the cause that leads on to the realization of event B. For instance, the relation of means and end is most distinctly expressed in exchange; at the same time, exchange personifies, as it were, the antagonistic character of such willing. The alien object is negated because it is alien, that is, because it belongs to somebody else; it is affirmed as possibly one's own. One's own object, on the other hand, is affirmed, its loss negated; but its relinquishment and transmission from one's own possession into that of another person are affirmed, not as an end, but as means to an end. The concept of arbitrary will appears in still greater perfection whenever the act of exchange is part of a combination of several such acts, as in trade, speculation, capitalistic production, in short, in every effort that aims at surplus value or net profit.

It is in the nature of the development of human thought that the type arbitrary will ascends to predominance over the type essential will. For if sensual perception already consists in comparison, so much more is this the case with the varieties of exact comparison, that is, the highly rational activities of measuring, weighing, and calculating, on which the arbitrary will is based. I therefore spoke of it as a form of thought more characteristic of men in contrast to women, of the aged in contrast to the young, and of the educated classes in contrast to the common people.

This contrast of the kinds of will, which my book works out in a variety of ways, hitherto has been utilized unsystematically in linguistics, poetry, biography, and history. I gave it a theoretical foundation for the first time. My treatment disregards ethical implications, however closely such implications may touch upon its content. Harald Hoeffding, who has examined my book most carefully, emphasizes "the calm objectivity with which it observes the phenomena of human life." At the same time, he underscores its "unique combination of sociology and psychology."[3] My only exception to the Danish philosopher's critique is that he makes too much of what he calls the author's "social pessimism." My pessimism refers to the future of the present civilization, not to the future of civilization itself.

My sole purpose was to point out the change which occurs in the relationship of man to man and of man to things, therefore also in the human will, when particular ideas come to be sharply distinguished from each other, that is, when they become entirely individual in character. It must be understood that they are never distinguished in perception, always in thought; never in reality, always in abstraction.

[3]   *Mindre Arbeider* (Copenhagen, 1899), pp. 142–57.

6

THE NATURE OF SOCIOLOGY

THE FACTS of human social life are the subject of scientific observation and knowledge at three levels.

As a rule, these three approaches are not being kept separate, and it is certainly not possible to do so absolutely. But neither are they being distinguished epistemologically, that is, properly understood conceptually, and yet this is not only possible but is a necessary requirement.

For one must distinguish (a) the biological, (b) the psychological, and (c) the strictly sociological view of the facts of human social life. The difference between the biological and the psychological views of the facts of social life is not difficult to comprehend.

Translated from the paper "Das Wesen der Soziologie" read before the Gehe Foundation, Dresden 1907; first published in *Neue Zeit- und Streit-fragen* IV, vol. 13, no. 9; reprinted in *Soziologische Studien und Kritiken* I, pp. 350–68. Slightly abridged. Subtitles are supplied by the editors. The reference in footnote 2 is to the Naples paper (1924) : cf. "The Divisions of Sociology," chap. 8 this volume.

In a note to the Gehe Foundation paper Toennies comments on the partial similarity of this paper and the paper presented at the Congress of Arts and Science—Universal Exposition, St. Louis 1904; cf. "The Present Problems of Social Structure," chap. 7 this volume. In Toennies' opinion the Gehe Foundation paper partly enlarges and partly modifies the St. Louis paper. Both papers are meant to affirm the theorems first elaborated in *Gemeinschaft und Gesellschaft* (1887) and also to refer critically to the position of Otto von Gierke, especially to his paper "Das Wesen der menschlichen Verbände" (Leipzig 1902). The St. Louis paper follows this paper.

We are entirely accustomed to looking at all organic beings, including man, as having a physis and a psyche; they are two sides of the
same thing. Consequently human social life, or the living together,
of men as well of other organisms is the object both of natural and
of spiritual analysis—if one may say so. Symbiosis among lower organisms is almost exclusively understood as being a natural event,
namely, a fact of mutual nourishment, assistance, and so forth;
naturalists are not intensively, or not at all, concerned with the
emotional life of animals and plants. This has something to do with
the fact that cognitive functions for a long time have been regarded
primarily as a thing of the intellect and, even more so, the human
mind as the normal mind—modes of thinking which are being
shed but slowly and with considerable difficulty. Of late, however,
a voluntaristic view is coming more and more to the fore, according to which drives and emotions are considered the universal
heritage of organic beings, including elementary organisms and
plants; the mind is then not a thing that somehow, in a puzzling
way, is "connected" with the body; rather, it is the essence of the
organism itself inasmuch as the organism exists by and of itself
and not merely in the perceptions of other minds.

We can of course observe the life of human beings, and consequently their social life, from the "outside," but it is only from the
"inside" that we can understand it; that is to say, we must interpret
it on the basis of self-knowledge, which teaches us that as a matter
of necessity human beings are determined by certain passionate
urges, by strong emotions that accompany the stimulation and the
restraint of such urges; and that human beings use their sense perceptions and, as a reservoir of their sense perceptions, their intelligence as guides, as scouts, as warners, so that they may discern
even from afar and in advance what is friendly or hostile, what is
favorable or dangerous. Thus, it is also complexes of feelings and
emotions that hold together human beings, and lead them to one
another—that "bind" them to each other, and hence "connect"
them. For they are not connected by an external physical cord, as
are, for example, two prisoners, who, with their wrists chained,
are being moved together. It is only metaphorically speaking that
there are psychological bonds, ties of love and friendship, unions

(*Verbindungen*) and associations (*Verbaende*) among human beings.

We know that the social and benevolent motives and thoughts are continually in contradiction and conflict with those of an opposite nature; that love and hate, trust and distrust, gratitude and vindictiveness cross one another; but also that fear and hope and, based on these emotions, human interests and intentions encounter each other, either in harmony or in disharmony, so that feelings as well as designs partly connect, partly divide human beings, singly as well as in groups of all kinds.

The psychological view of human social life regards attraction and repulsion, aid and combat, peaceful association and warlike conflict by themselves as equally important and relevant. The biological view is concerned with all such differences only because of the effect they have on increasing or reducing, stimulating or preventing life. The sociological view, as distinct from both, is essentially and in the first instance concerned with those facts that I call facts of reciprocal affirmation. Sociology investigates these specific and restricted social facts, analyzes their motives, and, in doing so, I maintain, must give particular attention to the difference whether reciprocal affirmation is based more on motives in feeling, or more on motives in reasoning; it must trace the process, which in this differentiation I design as the development from natural, or essential, will to rational, or arbitrary, will.

Essential will is volition as it has become, arbitrary will is volition as it is made. Man is by nature inclined toward affirmation of man, and therefore to union with him—not only through "instincts" (although instincts produce the strongest drives) but as much through "nobler" feelings and a reasonable consciousness. Out of the inclination arises volition (*Wollen*) and unequivocal affirmation, which recognizes the value of the object affirmed, and accordingly acts toward its full and durable affirmation. In the diverse forms this affirmation can take, the object is always affirmed directly or, as we say, as an end, that is, for its own sake. This does not, however, exclude its being affirmed at one and the same time also for another end, so long as the two ends remain in harmony and are reciprocally affirmative. Thus, the rider likes his horse; he does so because it is useful and it adds to his enjoyment; but he likes it, too, because he is immediately delighted with it; it gives him pleasure.

On the other hand, the idea of the end, the external purpose, may grow so strong that it causes affirmation of a means despite complete indifference toward its quality, therefore without arousing any pleasure; finally, notwithstanding a decided dislike. The dislike is being overcome, one forces himself to do, to take, to give something, although he does not care for it; he makes up his mind to do it because it appears to be the sensible (*vernuenftig*) thing to do. It is quite correct, and has often enough been discussed, that over a wide range an association and mixture of ideas may take place, by virtue of which the indifferent, even the loathsome, just because it is useful, may become acceptable and therefore I would say also be affirmed by essential will. Here is the location of that most important formation of essential will, which I indicate by the well-known term of habit, and which I relate to memory. This, however, is a secondary phenomenon, and there remains open a wide area, in which that association is not achieved but the original relation persists. The result is that even a single element which is affirmed by arbitrary will grows into a highly complex product or system—that is to say, a mechanism consisting in arbitrarily willed actions that are imagined and aforethought. Yet the nature of arbitrary will, as the nature of volition of any kind, is not restricted to action. It extends to anything that can be thought of as a means to human ends, and consequently may even extend to the whole nonself as the stuff for the desires, the aspirations, the interests of the self.

In the relation of one man to others, it is the arbitrary will, as understood here, that is relevant to the sociologist, whenever it can be thought of as reciprocally effective. In a unilateral way, it tends to treat the other as a thing or, as I prefer to say and did say, as stuff, while in the reciprocal relation, such tendencies are being balanced insofar as the other person is seen and accepted as a person, that is, as a subject endowed with arbitrary will. Consequently, one person may represent to another a mere means to his ends yet not be subjugated to these ends, in such a way that they remain free agents in relation to one another and are therefore capable of entering into a free relationship of reciprocal affirmation.

Even well-known sociologists are repeating ad nauseam the old thesis that man is by nature a social animal. But it is no more valid than the opposite thesis that, being by nature egotistic, or asocial, he becomes social as he makes reasoned judgments about his own well-understood interests; that he behaves socially only according to circumstances, that is, when and inasmuch as he thinks it will be to his advantage to come to terms and seek a working arrangement with his opponent—for to a degree, at least potentially, everyone is everyone's opponent.

I maintain that each of these opposite theses holds good, that each in its own area is valid and applicable, that they complement each other. The former is basic for the concept of *Gemeinschaft*, the latter for the concept of *Gesellschaft*.

This theorem of mine has often been understood to mean, and has so been interpreted, that these kinds were being distinguished in the same way the botanist distinguishes trees and grasses or the zoologist vertebrates and invertebrates. This is not my meaning. My method is comparable to that of the chemist rather than that of the descriptive natural sciences. It is a matter of isolation (*Scheidung*) rather than distinction (*Unterscheidung*). The point is to decompose the phenomenon of the social relation into its elements, and conceptually to set free these elements, whether or not their pure formation occurs in real life.

Social Relations

To conceptualize the social relationship is the first and fundamental scientific theme that essentially belongs to sociology.

We cannot discuss this theme without reference to those relationships that as legal relationships are the subject matter of a pure theory of civil law or of natural law in the old and true sense of the term.

The concept of social relationship is wider than that of the legal relationship. The legal relationship is a special category of the social relationship.

The really fundamental difference is to be found in the causes of the legal relationship. The first main cause of the relationship in private or civil law is *contract*, which is the prototype of a legal transaction with the object of doing something that has an effect in law. (Obligations arising from tort, that is, *ex delicto*, I would not count among immediate legal relationships). The other main cause is the natural condition, or status, of man, which today is of formal significance only in close family relationships. Not by contract but by status are we father or son, brother or sister, head of state or citizen, and on the basis of status have we certain subjective rights, or legal duties, with correlative subjective rights of others.

It is of the very nature of the legal relationship that the law, or the legal system, endows it with rights established by it and imposes duties originating in it. But entirely in analogy with the legal, we conceive of moral relationships, and talk of moral obligations and morally justified claims. Only on first appearance, however, is this concept as clear and straightforward as that of legal relationship. The truth of the matter is that, with regard to anything called moral, we never know without a specific indication whether this means something required by the mores, or by custom, or by positive morality as an accepted moral code which is closely related to custom, or, finally, by a generally accepted theological or philosophical system of ethics. This division produces at least three different species, or certain shadings, of moral relationships, even though most of them are subject equally to all three authorities and though, as a rule, all three agree about the norms that determine these relationships. Yet one has not far to seek for examples where those regulators, as they may be termed, diverge widely.

What in a specific sense of relationship is called an affair or a liaison between persons of different sex is being denied by custom and, as it were, passed over in silence. The legal system also ignores the "immoral" relationship. The accepted moral code, if independent from custom, at least puts up with it, provided that neither person is married, but derives scarcely any moral rights and duties from it—especially to the male partner who belongs to an upper social stratum it accords a degree of freedom and impudence which is indeed its—the accepted morality's—own disgrace. Theological ethics prefers to treat these things in the same way as custom. But a free and independent philosophical ethics will realize that the "immoral" relationship, though on principle ranking beneath the connubial and reprehensible when adulterous, may in special circumstances be equivalent to marriage in its moral nature and may in fact occasionally be superior in its moral value to many marital unions. But such ethics would, in all such cases, make exacting and serious demands in respect to the duties that arise from such a relationship, particularly for the male partner who belongs to a privileged social class—duties toward the woman, even when he discovers that she is not "worthy" of him, but most certainly duties toward their common offspring.

In whatever way one defines a moral relationship, it remains analogous to a legal relationship, in that an authority—if only, as in philosophical ethics, the autonomy of our practical reason—connects an "ought," or obligation (*ein Sollen*), with the relationship or derives such an obligation from it. Moral and legal relationships, therefore, are the subject matter of normative disciplines. But to conceptualize social relationships is the foremost task of a purely theoretical science of sociology. It differs from the natural sciences by virtue of the fact that its objects can neither be made visible by either telescope or microscope nor be perceived by the other senses. Only thought is capable of discerning them. They are a product of thought because they are abstracted from real life situations, that is, from the facts of social interaction. If we contemplate that at least the germs of a social relationship lie in all peaceful (or, as I have put it earlier, positive) conduct among human beings, and that conscious restraint from hostility represents such a germ, we have before the mind's eye the entire variety of sociological subject matter. The limitation to peaceful conduct, however, does not mean that forms of hostile conduct are irrelevant to the sociologist. They are, to be sure, as relevant to him as unorganized matter is relevant to the biologist or the physical states of matter are relevant to the chemist. It is the objects of research that are different in each.

It needs only a brief reflection to notice that social relationships to a large degree coincide with legal relationships, and that both those that coincide and those outside that field present in more than one sense a moral aspect. But even rights and obligations concern the sociologists first and foremost only insofar as they are actually perceived and thought of as such by the persons connected by these relations. And yet this way of looking at it is secondary in comparison with the study of real life conduct, in which the facts of social relationships are embedded.

Social Will

The second main theme of sociology, to which we now turn, is the field of social will and its products, for volition apart from the social context is a matter of psychology. In any social relationship there is present, albeit potentially, an element of social will, but its scope is far greater. The scope of social will is the whole of the environmental conditioning of social interaction. Custom and common law, religion and legislation, accepted usage (*Konvention*) and public opinion, style and fashion—all of them are expressions of different formations of social will. A simple and unambiguous instance of social will is a resolution passed commonly by a number of persons. The immediate content of a common resolution is that we intend to act in a certain way. Its content may be, too, that we want such and such to happen, something to be or become actual. And this occurrence or actualization may relate to others' acting or refraining from acting in some way. At this point we must take note of an important difference in what is meant by volition. The language constantly mixes up willing in the proper sense, which relates to one's doing something, with mere wishing. That something should happen, which is not the result of my own action, I can only wish. But to wish for something is very much like willing it, if I am determined to make it happen indirectly, more so if I am determined to force it into being, and still more so if I am capable of doing this. Wishing, then, merges into commanding.

Commands may emanate from single persons, or from several persons who have taken a common resolution. But they conform to the nature of social volition only, if the several persons are willing, hence enforcing their commands, and especially if they are capable of doing so. In circumstances such as these it does not matter, to begin with, for what reason the "others" obey, whether they are in a social relationship with those who command or whether they are subjected enemies or slaves. But the others can be these persons themselves as individuals, whose united volition forms the social volition which manifests itself as command. This is the most important case for sociological consideration: that human beings give themselves commands which they themselves obey—in commanding they perform a social action, in obeying they act as individuals.

Though most transparent when social volition takes the form of a resolution, social volition is no less important in its other formations. As I represent resolution as the type of rational volition, so do I represent habit as the type of irrational volition. That taking a resolution has both social and individual implications is self-evident; but it is no less manifest in the case of habit. As individual, man follows his habits; they control him, and he is often the "slave" of habit. In the same manner, people in the mass, though still individually, depend on habits with a social content, which we learn to discern as usage, custom, or common law; their extent and force increase as we delve in our researches into the life of the common people.

But how about habit—in what way is habit a social will? There appear to be two main reasons why this is not realized and accepted as the plausible explanation. The first has to do with the fact that self-reflection teaches us to understand volition as something that arises from reasoning, something that, as it were, is made, and being of our own making contrasts as something bright and lucid with our dark and unintended desires and urges. I do not mean to suggest that the concept of volition be fashioned in such a manner it comprises impulses and stirrings of the psyche, including those that remain unconscious. I would keep closer to linguistic meaning, and stress the perfect tense of volition in a linguistic sense —to will means literally to *have* made up one's mind, to *have* decided about something, and to *be* resolved. And how alive, even how necessary, this element in our concept is, language shows by creating variations of the word "to will," once this has worn off and become threadbare as an ordinary verb: such as "to be willing," "to be determined," "to be disposed," all of which are merely a refresher of the original sense, and can have no other function. It is this original sense that I extend in one direction, by drawing into my concept of volition also the being-used-to or being-in-the-habit-of, since it shares with the being-determined its essential criterion; namely the compelling destination toward an action, which is based on one's own inclination and one's own wish as the autonomous factor.

This leads directly to the second reason, which I think explains the failure to appreciate the point I have made, namely, the fact that reasoning must rely on linguistic usage, even when this is lax, indistinct, ambivalent. Language does indeed not discriminate between habit as an objective or, as one might put it, external fact and habit as a subjective, psychic or "internal" fact. The former usage, as external fact, contains nothing but the frequent repetition and regularity of acting and happening. But the latter conveys what we express when we say that habit is ingrown and has become our second nature and when we speak of the immeasurable influence that the habits of every person have on how he acts as well as on what he wishes and what he thinks, on his emotions and on his opinions. In the same way, we talk, without being aware of the difference of folk habits, of usages, of customs. They are indeed of interest as sheer facts of environment, as substantive processes; but in a quite different manner, and for the sociologist, they are far more immediately relevant as authoritative expressions of the folk spirit (*Volksgeist*), that is, as social will. In this latter meaning, custom has always been compared with law. Both of them possess validity, that is to say, they are of an ideal nature, they are a product of thought, demanding something that ought to be, and it needs a will to say that something ought to be.

Custom and formal law differ chiefly by their reasons. Custom states: because this is how it has always been, how it has always been done, practiced, considered proper. The formal law states: because this is what the legislator commands, and he commands it because he considers it correct and appropriate, and because he wishes to achieve something by the command. Opposition and conflict between custom and law manifest themselves mostly in the contest between common law, on the one hand, and statute law, on the other. No reminder is needed of the fact that formal statute law originates in resolution, in particular resolutions passed by assemblies.

So much about the contrast between resolution and habit; but the forms of the social as well as the individual will extend much further than that. An object of the greatest importance for sociological research is the religious creed, which is so closely connected with custom. Divine beings are not merely imagined and assumed beings, but as such they are, and are chiefly, beings that have been willed. The social will that posits them reveals itself not only by the faith in their existence, their power, their wrath, and their benevolence but even more so in the reverence devoted to them, in the temples and altars built to them, in sacrifices, and in all kinds of worship. They are creatures of folk imagery, and how else can something be made unless it is made by creative volition? They are, however, not only objects but, by virtue of that very fact, and thanks to the profusion and the ardor of the folk spirit, which, as it were, are being infused into them, they are subjects and bearers of the social will. As a rule they are being thought of as the zealous guardians of custom, chiefly because, and particularly so in the savage mind, they sternly insist on the observances, on receiving what is their due, in the image of despots and warlords. But they are also being thought of as legislators, or as inspiring the legislator. Though habits and titles are immutably valid, yet the god may change and renew them; his representatives on earth, in the name of god, whether they be called high priest or king, pope or emperor, may engage in free explanation and interpretative transformation of tradition, sacred though it be held in its substance. We owe valuable comments on these matters to Sir Henry Maine, a legal scholar who was able to think sociologically. But he, too, was unable to advance to the important insight that it is only different manifestations of social volition that are expressed in common law and sacred rights, on the one hand, and in freely conceived and planned legislation leaning on scientific theories, on the other.

For our unreflected awareness that which is, the actual reality, is indissolubly tied up with what is valid, and everything that is valid has its validity either for an individual alone through his individual will or for a number of individuals through their social will. The latter by far outweighs the former in significance. I recently published an essay I wrote nine years ago,[1] in which I have applied this truth to the meaning of words in common language and compared it to the validity of currency notes and coins. It is equally applicable to weights and measures, to chronology and epochs, to written signs and other symbols, to currently held views and opinions, particularly moral standards, to manners and etiquette—in short, to everything conventional. To appreciate what is conventional, and what is its scope, means to understand at least one major facet of the nature and the power of social volition.

We know, of course, that only in a few and relatively insignificant cases what is given validity by convention rests on an actual agreement that is like a contract. We say and assume, however, that there are many things so constituted *as though* they had been settled upon by agreement, and it is this feature that can best be indicated by the term "conventional." The term also connotes, in a minor key, something rigid and stiff, something artificial, therefore something frosty and cold. This connotation is a pointer to a highly significant difference in social volition whenever it establishes current values. The difference has its origin in a process from the internal toward externalization, from the organic to the mechanical agent, from essential will to arbitrary will—a process that takes place in the social as much as in the individual will. For custom and religion persist through that genuine warmth in emotion and imagination, that youthful naïve freshness, but also the innocence and childish folly of the common people's mind, or the folk spirit (*Volksgeist*). In the course of cultural development these motives are continually modified by matured experience, by increased knowledge, and by a more pronounced deliberateness in the pursuit of external ends. If they are, therefore, in part transformed and converted, in part challenged and abandoned, the im-

---

1   "Philosophical Terminology," *Mind* VIII N.S. pp. 289–332, 467–91 and IX N.S. pp. 46–61; *Philosophische Terminologie in psychologisch-soziologischer Ansicht* (Leipzig, 1906).

pulses of the process are particularly due to the influence of individual persons who distinguish themselves by intellectual freedom and a daring character.

The contradictions and conflicts between religion and science, between superstition and enlightenment are, no less than those between folk custom and the state police, between common law and statute law, the contradictions and conflicts between different and, indeed, opposed species or directions of social volition. The contradictions appear to indicate merely differences in thought and opinion; however, thoughts and opinions are backed up not only by the interests of classes and political parties but by different value systems called forth by changed circumstances; and in these value systems a more or less general volition crystallizes.

Social Unions

Of the scope and the implications of the problems located here, not much more than a faint idea can be conveyed in this outline. But the nature of sociology completes itself in its third main theme, where sociology breaks away even more decidedly than in the first two from biology and psychology, to enter a domain entirely its own. The third theme concerns the unions and associations among men, their fellowships and societies, communities and congregations, to name but a few of the general terms of those units, in the varieties of which pluralities of human individuals represent themselves. What is their essential nature? Are they something real or unreal? In what sense can they be the objects of scientific study? How are entities such as a race, a people, a nation, a tribe, a clan, a family, which also signify units in and above the pluralities, related to these categories? How are related to them the concepts of the state and of the church, which have gained such tremendous weight in all social life and its history? What are all these structures?

First of all, one must attend here to a significant difference, on which my whole exposition is based, that is, the difference between the various approaches to the study of human social life. For some of the units I have mentioned can be studied biologically, since their unity rests on natural facts of procreation and birth, descent and hereditary characteristics, while at the same time they are imbued with a psychological valuation as units that are carriers of social ideas. To inquire into their reality would mean to renew the old controversy between realism and nominalism; this has been settled in modern science with hardly an exception in favor of nominalism, which holds that only what we call single things are real. To discuss this matter here falls outside my plan for this paper. But, since it all too often has been completely disregarded or badly neglected, I must emphatically underline the distinction between such biological and at best psychological universals and groups, on the one hand, and the actual social wholes or, preferably, social bodies, on the other. Only with these are we concerned here and now, although there is every reason to keep in mind the former, when occasion arises, and to heed certain points of contact between the two fundamentally different genera.

A social union has, in the first instance and immediately, something like an existence only through the united, therefore, social will of the persons that belong to it, as and when they posit the union in their minds. As a rule this truth is being expressed by the statement that a social union is a fiction. This expression, however, is regularly applied only in jurisprudence. The jurist talks of corporate persons that exist besides natural persons or individuals, and he explains them as a fiction created for specific purposes by the law or the legislator. The sociologist is interested in a much wider range of human units, and it does not matter at first whether or not they have been recognized in a legal system as bearers of rights and obligations, just as it was of no significance to us whether or not a social relationship also appears in the form of a legal relationship. Trade unions and workingmen's federations have not yet (1907) been endowed with the legal status of a corporate person; even less so political parties or associations. Does this mean that they do not exist? Are they not extremely important formations in our present-day social environment? Whereby, then, do they exist?

They do exist, (1) and chiefly, through the will of their members who have established such an association or, like its founders, assume and affirm it by their performance. They furthermore exist (2) through being taken notice of and given recognition on the part of other individuals and associations, especially their equals; and (3), for the spectator and theorist, as he takes note of these modes of existence, and distinguishes them from other modes of existence. But obviously the first *ratio essendi* is the fundamental one, and the others depend on it. We know that any group of persons can call into being an association, if they will it in common and can agree on it, and in doing so they perform an act of pretense or fiction. For at first it is in their imagination only, in their idea, but dependent on their volition, that the association exists; and they have a common purpose the association is meant to serve.

The association can achieve this purpose by its mere existence, that is, by being construed—and as it is being construed, it receives a name—but as a rule it must be capable of a will of its own, it must be capable of being represented, and the agreement, which legally is called the articles of association, must settle how the representative will is to be formed: thus the association is given its constitution. This simple, logically lucid instance is known to all of us by experience. The question arises whether this concept of association can provide the standard for measuring all species of human units. What has, in the context of this question, made the greatest stir is the question whether even the state, or the government, can and ought to be conceived of as an association. This is the problem of the social contract.

The Age of Enlightenment unanimously believed, and, what is more, was convinced it knew and had clearly and unmistakably understood, that the state was based on contracts. The nineteenth century, which in its main currents of thought was an age of restoration, destroyed this belief and this certainty; yet it produced in its turn no generally accepted political theory. Initially it was history that was being appealed to, and the historical school of law staked its claim against natural law. States, it was claimed, had in reality originated everywhere, or only with insignificant exceptions, in ways other than by contracts, and until this day this plausible truth has been echoed vividly enough. Against it, one may refer to Kant, who had made it abundantly clear that what the contract theory was about was the idea of the thing but not the question of the historic origin. To everyone who knows natural law theory and the philosophy at its root, this is downright self-evident. Yet, it is retorted, the origin, the development, the historical being-as-it-has-become, are all that counts; they are the only instrument with which to grasp the nature of the thing. Whose nature? Well, the state's. And what precisely is the sort of thing the state is? Well, something that has developed, that is to say, a living thing, an organism.

At this point, the resistance against the natural law concept of the state joins up with a school of thought that, by now precariously surviving among natural scientists, has been eagerly embraced by modern sociology. Among the sociologists, however, the chief interest lies with "society" or "the social body" rather than with the state. Whatever its particular shape, this view is opposed to the individualistic view of social life. I do not defend this individualistic view. But I do maintain that the subsumption under the concept of organism, whether of society at large or of the state, contains a tangle of misconceptions, and I refer back to what I have already strongly underlined, that is, the difference between objects of research in biology and sociology. I do maintain that conceptualistic realism (as defined more recently) should, as far as organic beings are concerned, not be dismissed as easily as, curiously enough, this is being done by those selfsame natural scientists, to whom the application of the concept of organism to social formations seems to be the most natural and most evident thing under the sun. I accept as valid, in fact, I set great store by, the insight that a people, a race, a family as biological phenomena exist as a reality in the exact meaning of the term, difficult though it may be to define that reality precisely. In other words, they must, and certainly may, be understood as real beings since we cannot but ascribe to them the essential criteria of life, such as in particular the self-preservation of the whole by the elimination of old and the reproduction of new parts. But all the more energetically I must emphasize the theory that social entities or unions and associations among men are of an essentially ideal (*ideell*) nature; that they are a product of thought in the sense that the very fact of their being entities entirely depends upon the minds of their members, of whom one can rightly state what Bishop Berkeley applied to the whole of the external world: *esse* = *percipi* (to be is to be perceived). For all that, I attribute to them, as much as the metaphysical idealist attributes to matter as such, a certain empirical reality: it is that social reality which is grounded in the ideas about them, hence in the minds of men. This is why I say that the sociological view of life follows, and depends on, the psychological view, as the psychological view follows and depends on the biological.

As social unions, so social relations and social will and the values posited by it exist only and insofar as they are perceived, felt, imagined, thought, known, and willed, primarily by individuals. Does there exist, then, such a thing as a folk mind, a natural consciousness, a common and united feeling and thinking? Whether some such thing does exist, except in the agreement among individuals and the harmony in their feelings and thoughts, is a problem that once more leads back to conceptualistic realism. The problem is a different one in relation to material things, a different one in relation to the mind (*Seele*). If it is accepted for organisms, it is hardly possible not to accept it with regard to the mind. For organisms, as live matter, as I have said earlier, *are* mind rather than merely connected with mind; the mind is located in the organism. The fact of the matter is that organisms must be understood as matter and mind at one and the same time. If, as I believe, thinking and willing exist as objective reality, then especially those formations of social will that are so close to it—social habit, social belief, custom, and religion—are something entirely different, depending on whether they are considered in this, their objective reality (which they possess by virtue of being subjective entities), or in their subjective, or as we now prefer to say, their social reality; therefore, as ideally constructed objective entities. However, this somewhat intricate point need not concern us here any further.

I repeat that, at any rate, as all unions among men, communities, fellowships, corporations, and so forth, so is the state something that is ideally constructed. The remaining question is, then, of what kind this ideational element is and how it can be conceptualized. With this question we return to the contrast in the concepts of essential will and arbitrary will, *Gemeinschaft* and *Gesellschaft*. The state can be experienced and thought of by its own subjects, its citizens, and its people, as essential purpose, therefore as being alike to an organism or a natural whole, which comprises all those who know themselves dependent on it and conditioned by it, whose members they are, and which by its very nature exists before they exist. Here is the seat of the connection with the biological view, the conceptualistic realism, and the theory of organism. For it goes without saying that in its psychological implications this view is easier and more likely to be adopted when any unions thus constructed are identical with natural wholes, or at least as similar as may be; if—to put it plainly—for example, the state possesses a close likeness to the family (considered as a social entity) and the family as a social entity is a reminder of the family as we know it from natural history.

This last condition is most nearly satisfied in a social union whose special basis is consanguinity and common descent. The family, in its two varieties of patriarchal or matriarchal domination (*Herrschaft*) and of fraternal-egalitarian fellowship (*Genossenschaft*), is therefore the type of *Gemeinschaft* based on essential will. But in its further development, particularly under the impact of urban civilization, this structure moves far away from its type and ceases to be like a family that carries its own purpose in itself in all its naturalness and inevitability; it comes to resemble more and more an association, which has an external purpose and is essentially a means to achieve the expressed or unexpressed, open or latent ends of its founders and members—from which we started as from the clearest and most rational social entity. The association is the type of *Gesellschaft*, which has sprung from free rational, or arbitrary, will, whether actually or in its intention. *Gemeinschaft*, I repeat, assimilates to the rational purpose—association. But against this must be held the possibility that *Gemeinschaft* may remain, and continue to develop as *Gemeinschaft*, if the corresponding way of thinking and its social will gains the support of new aids; if, for example, the whole or the commonwealth, though no longer and less and less like a natural union, or a quasi-organic whole, yet portrays itself as such an entity in emotion, imagination, and reflective thought, that is to say, if the common spirit wants to maintain it as such.

It is here in particular that the inestimable influence of religion on social life lies, and one might say even more specifically on political life. This influence is preserved despite the fact that gradually, with the scientific outlook advancing and faith, whether for this or any other reason, decaying, religion must content itself with a mere role, which it plays under the masks of its priests and other dignitaries. The idea remains the same: the commonwealth is being hallowed and raised above criticism; it is being thought of as a god, or the special emanation of a god, whether this godly loftiness and grace are effused over the person and the inherited rights of a sovereign or live forth in the tutelary genius of a city community. What matters is that, with the statute and the law also their originators, interpreters and transformers are being lifted to the supranatural glow of beings to whom reverence is owed. Consequently, the social union, whether called the state or by any other name, exercises that higher authority, or lays claim to it, over the individual subjects and citizens, which a creator claims over his creatures, a mother over her children, whom she has nourished at her bosom. But then it is fatal indeed if religious consciousness brings forth, as it were, from its own powers a community as a *Civitas Dei*, in opposition to the worldly commonwealth, which in turn is being stigmatized as temporal and profane, if not as *Civitas Diaboli*—the Church against the Empire, which now must borrow its godly attributes from the Church.

That the Church is of godly origin is self-evident to the faithful. But is the empire, or even the city community? With the deities of its citadel, the Hellenic *polis* was a place of pious faith and cult. The modern city could never quite gain such intrinsic exaltedness, notwithstanding the fact that in the last century three or four cities were misshaped in the caricature of a sovereign member of the German federal system. The old German empire, as is known, remained until its demise the Holy Roman Empire.

What we must try to understand is that for the actual nature of the state or of any other community, in particular one that is not specifically ecclesiastic, the decisive criterion is the economic relation of the whole to its parts, in other words, the rights of ownership. Can private property be construed—and is it in its chief functions such that it can legitimately be so construed—as independent, free in its own right, as though the people, some with their capital and their land, some with their naked bodies, had entered into the state, and concluded the social contract in the same manner in which the captain of industry or the lord of the manor contracts on the basis of formal equality with people offering their labor as a commodity? Or, is it true that one must construe the state as a guardian angel, who attends to the distribution of wealth according to the principles of merit and justice, and then grants the one an annual income of two to five million, the other an income of one hundred or two hundred dollars?

I cannot enter, at this stage, into a discussion of this problem. No simple answer is possible, but it will be understood that here I am touching on the problem of socialism. This problem can, as a matter of fact, be formulated thus: whether social volition and reflection in our time will prove strong enough to develop the modern state into a genuine community (*Gemeinschaft*) which extends to the mastery over private property—perhaps, instead of "to develop," one ought to say "to transform"; or, whether the tendencies of *Gesellschaft* will remain preponderant in this social volition and reflection.

With these comments on the three objects of knowledge—social relations, social will, social unions,[2] I hope I have succeeded in expressing exhaustively the essential nature of sociology.

To be sure, concerning social relations, the sociological approach remains closely connected with related approaches in biology and psychology. But concerning social volition and social un-

---

2   The triadic division of the objects of knowledge in pure sociology has more recently been re-formulated, so that social will is replaced by "collectives" ("*Samtschaften*"), which in the same manner as relations and corporations (unions) represent a species of social bonds. Social will, apart from its being treated in social psychology, is then subordinated to these species of social bond, as being conditioned by them.

ions, while connections with psychology are evident, the subject matter of sociology is of a particular nature, because it is conditioned by reason and thought; it is therefore meaningless to speak of "states" of bees and ants. The social life of animals can be approached biologically and psychologically, but one cannot in the least assume that their social relations, their common volition, and especially their unions are objects to them; and because this is so only with regard to humans, it can be stated that this *Trias* is the natural and necessary subject matter of a conceptual, that is, a theoretical or philosophical science of sociology.[3]

Sociology is confronted by the vast profusion of social, and that means also historical, life. Its task is to take hold of it through its categories, to stir it up, and to saturate itself with it, in order to ascertain what its patterns are, and at least to conjecture its wherefrom and whereto. For scientific knowledge about it can be achieved but only in dim outline. It ought to be added that history is not a separate science. The writing of history is a profound art, resting though it does on the search for truth, which must be undertaken in the scientific spirit. She has her own rules, her glorious tradition, her celebrated masters. It is not surprising that she refuses to accept new standards, let alone prescriptions, from an immature sociology. Applied sociology's task is not to compete with the writing of history. It is nothing but the philosophy of history, however little or much that may be thought to involve. But this should certainly be fashioned in such a way that the historian may learn from it, indeed, cannot help but learn from it. The main body of philosophy, in the course of the last few centuries, has been transforming itself more and more from a theological into a secular-scientific synopsis and synthesis. On this road the philosophy of history has so far remained farthest behind. The theological world view has sought and found its fulfillment in a philosophy of history. The scientific world view, likewise, must be consummated in the philosophy of history.

[3]   This paragraph is a summary of somewhat more extensive statements in the text.—EDS.

7

THE PRESENT PROBLEMS OF

SOCIAL STRUCTURE

THE PROBLEMS of social structure we find in a rather confused state at the present moment. In an earlier stage of sociological
thinking, considerable expectations were attached to the interpretation of social phenomena by means of biological analogies or
what was called the organic theory of society. These expectations
may now be said to have been disappointed. The organic theory
has almost universally been abandoned. Yet even its severest
critics are likely to admit that there is some truth in or behind it,
although they seem to be at a loss to explain properly what kind
of truth it is.

By a curious coincidence, the three most notable representatives of that doctrine—the Russian Paul von Lilienfeld, a man of
high social standing; the German Albert Schaeffle, with a reputation as a political economist; and the Englishman Herbert Spencer, whose fame needs not to be emphasized—all departed from
life in the year 1903, the two latter in the month of December; all
in advanced old age. To these three men sociology owes a debt of
gratitude, because, after Comte, they were the first—at least in
Europe—to formulate a theory of social life in large outline. From

From "The Present Concept of Social Structure." *American Journal of
Sociology* 10, no. 5 (March 1905) : 569–88. The paper was read at the
Congress of Arts and Science, St. Louis, September 1904. It appears that
Toennies was invited to the Congress by its two Vice-Presidents, Hugo
Muensterberg, Professor of Psychology, Harvard University, and Albion
Small, Professor of Sociology, University of Chicago. The other speakers
in the section "Social Structure," where Toennies delivered his paper,
were Gustav Ratzenhofer and Lester F. Ward.

all, but especially from Schaeffle and Spencer, we receive, and shall continue to receive, constant and fertile impulses or sug- gestions. But I feel safe in predicting that it will soon be universally acknowledged that the foundations of their theories were not laid firmly enough for permanently supporting those boldly planned structures of thought.

For a long time past I have cherished the opinion that these authors, as well as nearly all their successors and critics, are ham- pered by a fundamental lack of clearness as to the subject of their inquiries—a subject which they are in the habit of designating by the very indefinite name of "a society," or, as Schaeffle puts it, "*the* social body." Confusion of ideas invariably proceeds from a defect of analytical reasoning; that is to say, of proper distinction.

I believe and assert that three distinct conceptions, the com- mon object of which is social life in its broadest sense, are not sufficiently, or not at all, kept apart nor even recognized as being distinct, namely, the biological, the psychological, and the socio- logical in what I call the exclusive sense, the subject of only this third conception being entirely new, as compared with the sub- jects of other sciences or departments of philosophy. It seems to me to be our fundamental task as philosophical sociologists to de- duce from this last conception, and others implied in it, a system of social structure which shall contain the different notions of col- lective entities in their mutual dependence and connection; and I firmly trust that out of such a system will be gained a better and more profound insight into the evolution of society at large, and into its historical phases, as the life of these collective entities. It is therefore in the struggles, first, between any of these groups and the individuals composing it; second, between their different forms and kinds—for instance, the struggles between Church and empire; between Church and cities; between Church and state; between cities and other corporations; between the sovereign state and feudal communities, and consequently established orders or es- tates; between single states and a federal state—it is in these and similar struggles, presupposing the *existence* of those collective entities, that the growth and decay of higher civilizations exhibit themselves most markedly.

I

When we speak of a house, a village, or a city, the idea immediately arising in our minds is that of a visible building; or of larger and smaller groups of buildings; but soon we also recollect the visible contents of these buildings, such as rooms and cellars and their furniture; or, when groups of buildings are concerned, the roads and streets between them. The words "house," "village," and "city" are, however, used in a different sense when we have in mind the particular contents of buildings which we call their inhabitants, especially their human occupants. Very often, at least in many languages, people are not only conceived of as the inhabitants of, but as identical with, the buildings. We say, for instance, "the entire house," "the whole village"—meaning a lot of people the idea of whom is closely connected with the idea of their usual dwelling place. We think of them as being one with their common habitation. Nevertheless it is still a visible union of individuals which we have in mind. This visible union, however, changes into an invisible one when it is conceived of as lasting through several generations. Now the house will become identified with a family or perhaps with a clan. In the same manner, a village community or a township will be imagined as a collective being, which—although not in all, yet in certain important, respects—remains the same in essence, notwithstanding a shifting of matter; that is to say, an incessant elimination of waste portions—men who die—and a constant accretion of fresh elements—children, who are born. Here the analogy with the essential characteristics of an organism is obvious. Vegetable and animal organisms likewise are only represented by such elements as are visible at any time, and the law of life consists in this, that the remaining portions always predominate over the eliminated and the reproduced ones, and that the latter by and by move and fill up the vacant spaces, while the relations of parts—for example, the cooperation of cells as tissues, or of tissues as organs—do not undergo a substantial change. Thus such an application of biological notions to the *social life* of mankind—as the organicist theories or methods set out to do

—is not to be rejected on principle. We may, in fact, look upon any community of this kind—maintaining itself by renewing[1] its parts—as being a living whole or unity. This view is the more plausible if the renewal itself is merely biological, as indeed is the case in the human family, and, as we think, to a still greater extent —because a family soon disperses itself—in certain larger groups; a tribe, a nation, or a race; although there is involved in this view the question whether there is a sameness of nature—or, as we usually say, of blood—guaranteed, as it should be, by inbreeding (German: *Inzucht*).[2] Indeed, this self-conservation of a group is the less to be expected, the smaller the group; and it is well known among breeders that it is necessary for the life of a herd not to continue too long selecting sires of the same breed, but from time to time to refresh the blood by going beyond the limits of a narrow parentage and by crossing the race by mixtures with a different stock.

At any rate, this is what I should call a purely *biological* aspect of collective human life, insofar as their conception is restricted to the mere existence of a human group, which, so to speak, is self-active in its maintenance of life.

This aspect, however, does not suffice when we consider social units of a local character, which also continue their existence, partly in the same, but partly in a different, manner. With reference to them, we do not think exclusively of a natural *Stoffwechsel*, as it is effected by births and deaths of the individuals composing the body, but we also consider the moving to and fro of living men, women, and children, the ratio of which, like the ratio of births and deaths, may cause an incerase or a decrease of the whole mass, and *must* cause one or the other if they do not balance. In consequence of this, we also have less reason to expect a biological identity of the stock of inhabitants at different times than a lasting connection between a part of space (the place), or rather a piece

---

[1]   The original has "receiving," obviously a misreading of Toennies' manuscript.—EDS.

[2]   The original has "in-and-in breeding of parents." That T. does not mean inbreeding in the pathological sense is clear from the subsequent sentence.—EDS.

of the soil, and a certain group of men who dwell in that place and have intercourse with each other, although the place itself grows with the number of its inhabitants, and although even among these inhabitants there may be, for instance, not one direct descendant of those who occupied the place say, a hundred years ago. We may, it is true, take it to be the rule that at least a certain nucleus of direct descendants keeps alive through many generations—a rule so much more certain if it is a large place, a whole region, or even a country that we have in mind. Still, we shall not hold this to be a *conditio sine qua non* for acknowledging the village or the city to be the same; it being in this respect much more relevant that the nucleus of the place, of the "settlement," has endured and has preserved itself through the ages. Now, since place and region, air and climate, have a very considerable effect upon the intelligence and sentiment of the inhabitants, and since a considerable change may not justly be expected with respect to this, except when the minds as well as the external conditions of the newcomers are totally different from those of the older strata, we may consider the identity of a place, insofar as it is founded upon the social connection of men with a part of the soil, as a *psychological* identity, and call this aspect of social life a psychological aspect. There can be no doubt that this psychological aspect is in great part dependent upon the biological aspect and is, as a rule, closely interwoven with it. Yet it needs but little reflection to recognize that both are also to a certain extent separate and independent of each other. The subject matter of a social psychology is different from the subject matter of a social biology, though there exist a great many points of contact between them, and though both, apart from the foundations here given to them, may be applied to animal as well as to human societies.

II

Neither of the above-mentioned conceptions of a continuous unity or whole implies that the essential characteristic of the unity is perceived and recognized by those who belong to it, much less that it is perceived by others, by outsiders. And this is the

third idea, by far the most important one for the present consideration—the idea of what I propose to designate by the name of a
corporation, including under it all social units whatever, insofar
as they have this trait in common—that the mode of existence of
the unity or whole itself is founded upon the consciousness of its
existence, and consequently that it perpetuates itself by the conception of its reality being transmitted from one generation to the
next one; which will not happen unless it is done on purpose by
teaching, and generally in the form of tradition. This evidently
presupposes human reason and human will, marking off sharply
this third genus from any kind of animal subhuman society.

We are now going to give closer attention to this conception.
For the most part, though not always, it is the conception of a
unity different from the aggregate of members; the idea of a psy-
chical or moral *body*, capable of willing and of acting like a single
human being; the idea of a self or person. This person, of course,
is an artifical or fictitious one. It represents indeed, as the former
two conceptions did, a unity persisting through the change of its
parts, but this unity and identity persisting in the multitude are
neither biological nor directly and properly psychological, but
must, in distinction from these, be considered as specifically *sociological;* that is to say, while the second is the social consciousness
or social mind itself, this is the product of it, and can be understood only by looking into the human soul, and by perceiving
thoughts and wills which not only have a common drift and
tendency but are creators of a common work.

The idea, however, of a body capable of willing and acting is,
as said above, not always, and not necessarily, implied in the idea
of a sociological unit. This is a conception preceding it, as proto-
plasm precedes individual bodies; namely, the general idea of a
society (or a community, if this important distinction is adverted
to), which is not essentially different from our second idea of a
psychological unit, except in this one respect, accessory to it, that
the idea of this unit be present somehow in the minds of the people
who feel or know themselves as belonging to it. This conception is
of far-reaching significance, being the basis of all conceptions of
a social, as contrasted with a political, corporation. It therefore

comprises especially those spheres of social life which are more or less independent of political organization, among which the economic activity of men is the most important, including, as it does, domestic life as well as the most remote international relations between those who are connected exclusively by the ties of commercial interest. But practically it is of little consequence whether this general idea be considered as psychological or as sociological, unless we precisely contemplate men who consciously maintain their own conception of their own social existence, in distinction from other ideas relating to it, chiefly when it is put in contrast to the idea of a political corporation, and the political corporation of highest import is concerned—the state. And it was exactly in these its shifting relations to the state that the idea of society proper—though without recognition of its subjective character—was evolved about fifty years ago by some German theorists—notably Lorenz Stein, Rudolph Gneist, and Robert Mohl—who were more or less strongly under the sway of Hegelian philosophy, seeing that Hegel in his *Rechtsphilosophie* develops his idea of human corporate existence under the threefold heading of (1) the family as "thesis," (2) civil society as "antithesis," and (3) the state as "synthesis" of the two former.

But, though I myself lay considerable stress upon this general notion of society, in juxtaposition and opposition to the state or political society, I still regard it as more indispensable to a theory of social structure to inquire into the nature and causes of what may be called, from the present point of view, genuine corporations; that is, those conceived of as being capable of willing and acting like a single individual endowed with reason and self-consciousness. The question arises how a "moral person" may be considered as possessing this power.

Evidently this is an impossibility, unless one single individual or several together are willing and acting *in the name of* that fictitious being. And in order justly to be taken for the volitions and acts of an individual distinct from their own individualities, those volitions and acts must be distinguishable by certain definite marks from the rest of their willing and acting, which they do in their own name; they must be differentiated formally. There must be a tacit or an open understanding, a sort of covenant or convention, that only volitions and acts so differentiated shall be considered as volitions and acts of the said moral person whom one or those several individuals are supposed to represent. By the way, this question of marks and signs, consensual or conventional, by which a thing, physical or moral, not only is recognized as such but by which its value (or what it is *good for*) is differentiated from its existence (or what it *is*), pervades all social life and mind, and may be called the secret of it. It is clear that certain signs may easily be fixed or invented whereby the volitions and acts of a single individual may be differentiated from the rest as being representative. But how if there are more than one, who only occasionally have one will and act together, and who cannot be supposed to agree in their feelings as soon as they are required to represent their moral person? It is well known that these must be "constituted" as an *assembly* or as a whole capable by its constitution to deliberate and, what is more, to resolve and act. It must be settled by their own or by the will of another person (1) under what conditions, and with respect to what subject matters, their resolutions shall be considered as representing declarations of will of their own body; and (2) under what conditions, and with respect to what subject matters, declarations of will of this body shall be valid as declarations of will of the moral person they represent.

It is therefore the *constitution* of a multitude into a unity which we propose as a fourth mode, and as a necessary consequence of the third one, unless the moral person be represented exclusively by a single man or woman as a natural person. The many constitute themselves or are constituted as a body, which is, as far as it may be, similar to a natural person in such relations as are essential precisely for the notion of a person. Consequently, this body also is a unity, but a unity conceived a priori as being destined for a definite purpose, namely, the representation of a moral person— the third or sociological kind of unity. And it is different from that third notion only by this very relation, which evidently cannot be inherent in that person himself. That, in consequence of this relation, it has a visible existence apart from its own idea, while the moral person represented is nothing beyond his own idea. We may distinguish, therefore, between five modes of existence in a moral person represented by a body: (1) the ideal existence in the minds of its members; (2) the ideal existence of the body constituted, which represents the moral person, being as well in the minds of the natural persons who compose that body as in the minds of members of the corporation generally; (3) the visible existence of this body, being the assembly of natural persons, willing and acting under certain forms; (4) the intelligible existence of this assembly, being conditioned by a knowledge, on the part of those who externally or theoretically perceive it, of its constitution and its meaning; (5) the intelligible existence of the moral person or the body represented, being conditioned of a knowledge of the relation between this corporation and the body representing it, implying the structure of the former in the first, and of the latter in the second instance.

The visible existence of an assembly means that members are visible as being assembled, but the assembly as a body can be recognized only by a reflecting spectator who knows what those forms mean, who "realizes" their significance, who *thinks* the assembly. Of course, a corporation also, apart from its representation, can be perceived only mentally, by outsiders as well as by its own members, and these are different perceptions (distinguished here as ideal and intelligible existence): members perceiving it directly as a product of their own will, and therefore in a way as their property (a thing which they own); and outsiders perceiving it only indirectly, by knowing the person or body that represents it; this being an external perception only, unless it be supplemented by a knowledge of its peculiar mode of being, that is, of its constitution and of the relations which members bear to the whole, and the whole to its members.

But it is, above all, in this respect that great differences exist between different kinds of corporations. The first question is whether individuals feel and think themselves as founders or authors or at least as representative ideal authors of their own corporation. Let us take an obvious example. Suppose a man and a woman contract a marriage (we waive here all questions of church or state regulations for making the marriage tie public). They are said to found a family. Now, the children springing from this union and growing up in this family cannot justly feel and think themselves as the creators or authors of it as long as they are dependent upon their parents. However, they partake of it more and more consciously, and some day they may take upon themselves the representation of this whole internally and externally, in place of their father and mother. They may learn to feel and to think of themselves as bearers of the personality of this ideal being, playing, so to speak, the parts of the authors and founders, whom they also may survive and will survive in the normal course of human events; and they may continue the identity of the family beyond the death of their parents. They may maintain the continuity of this identical family, even when new families have sprung from it which may or may not regard themselves as members of the original one. The proposition that it exists still is true at least for those who will its truth and who act upon this principle; nay, it is by their thought and will that they are creating it anew as it was made originally by the wills of the first two persons. A different question is whether the existence of this corporation will be recognized and acknowledged by others who may stand in relation to its members or may simply be impartial theoretical spectators.

But, further, there is this fundamental difference in the relation of individuals to that ideal entity which they think and will, whether they be its real or merely its representative authors, namely: (1) they may look upon the corporation, which they have created really or ideally, as upon a thing existing for its own sake, as an end in itself, although it be at the same time a means for other ends; or (2) they may conceive it clearly as a mere tool, as nothing but an instrument for their private ends, which they either naturally have in common or which accidentally meet in a certain point.

The first case appears in a stronger light if they consider the social entity as really existing, and especially if they consider their corporation as a living being; for a real thing, and especially a living thing, has always some properties of its own. The latter has even something like a will of its own; it cannot be conceived as being disposable, divisible, applicable, and adaptable at pleasure to any purpose, as a means to any end—this being the notion of pure matter, as it exists only in our imagination; and therefore a thing which has merely nominal existence would be really nothing but a mass of such imaginary matter, absolutely at one's disposal, offering no resistance, being stuff in itself, that is to say, potentially anything one may be able to make, to knead, to shape, or to construe out of it (of course real matter may and will more or less approach to this idea). On the other hand, to think of an ideal thing as being ideal is not the same as to think of it as imaginary matter; but if one aims at a certain object, if one follows out one's designs, one is constrained by a psychological necessity to break resistances and to subject things as well as [other] wills to one's own will; one tends to make them all alike, as "wax in one's hand," to remove or to oppress their own qualities and their own wills, so as to leave, as far as possible, nothing but a dead and unqualified heap of atoms, a something of which imaginary matter is the prototype. Of course, it is only as a tendency that this dissolving and revolutionary principle is always active, but its activity is manifest everywhere in social life, especially in modern society, and characterizes a considerable portion of the relations of individuals to each other and consequently to their corporations.

As long as men think and regard "society"—that is to say, their clan or their polis, their church or their commonwealth— as real and as truly existing; nay, when they even think of it as being alive, as a mystical body, a supernatural person, so long will they not feel themselves as its masters; they will not be likely to attempt using it as a mere tool, as a machine for promoting their own interests; they will look upon it rather with awe and humility than with a sense of their own interest and superiority. And, in consequence of feelings of this kind, they even forget their own authorship—which, as a rule, will indeed be an ideal one only; they will feel and think themselves not creators but creatures of their own corporations. This is the same process as that which shows itself in the development of men's regular behavior toward their gods, and the feeling and thinking just mentioned are always closely related to, or even essentially identical with, religious feeling and thinking. Like the gods themselves, to whom so regularly *la cité antique,* with its temples and sanctuaries, is dedicated, the city or corporation itself is supposed to be a supernatural eternal being, and consequently existing not only in a real but in an eminent sense.

But, of course, all feelings of this kind are but to a limited extent liable to retard the progress of a consciousness of individual interests, or, as it is commonly spoken of—with a taint of moral reproach—of selfishness. As a matter of fact, it is the natural ripening of consciousness and thinking itself which makes reflection prevail over sentiment, and which manifests itself, first and foremost, in reflection upon a man's own personal interest in the weighing and measuring of costs and results; but, second, also in a similar reflection upon some common interest of business which a person, from whatever motive, selfish or not, has made his own affair; and third, in that unbiased interest and in reflection upon the nature and causes of things and events, of man's happiness and social existence, which we call scientific or philosophical.

All reflection is, in the first instance, analytical. I have spoken already of the dissolving principle which lies in the pursuing of one's own personal affairs, of which the chase after profit is but the most characteristic form. But the same individualistic standpoint is the standpoint, or at least the prevailing tendency, of science also. It is *nominalism* which pervades science and opposes itself to all confused and obscure conceptions, closely connected as it is with a striving after distinctness and clearness and mathematical reasoning. This nominalism also penetrates into men's supposed collective realities (supernatural or not), declaring them to be void and unreal, except insofar as individual and real men have consented to make such an artificial being, to construct it, and to build it up mentally. Knowledge and criticism oppose themselves to faith and intuition, in this as in most other respects, and try to supplant them. To know how a church or a state is created means the downfall of that belief in its supernatural essence and existence which manifestly is so natural to human feeling and intellect. The spirit of science is at the same time the spirit of freedom and of individualistic self-assertion, in contradiction and in opposition to the laws and ties of custom—as well as of religion, so intimately connected and homologous with custom—which seem entirely unnatural and irrational to analytical reasoning. This reasoning always puts the questions: What is it good for? Does it conduce to the welfare of those whom it pretends to bind or to rule? Is it in consonance with right reason that men should impose upon themselves the despotism of those laws and of the beliefs sanctioning them?

The classical answer has been given in a startling fashion by one whom Comte called the father of revolutionary philosophy. There is, says Thomas Hobbes, a realm of darkness and misery, founded upon superstition and false philosophy, which is the Church; and there is, or there might be, a realm of light and happiness, founded upon the knowledge of what is right and wrong; that is to say, of the laws of nature, dictated by reason and by experience, to check hostile and warlike individual impulses by a collective will and power; this realm is the true state, that is to say, the idea and model of its purely rational structure, whether it may exist anywhere as yet or not. Hobbesianism is the most elaborate and most consistent system of the doctrine commonly known as that of natural law (*Naturrecht*), including, as it always did, a theory of the state. As a matter of fact, this doctrine has been abandoned almost entirely, especially in Germany, where it had been exerting a very considerable influence in the century which preceded the French Revolution, when even kings and absolutist statesmen were among its open adherents. It has been controverted and abandoned ever since the first quarter of the nineteenth century—a fact which stands in manifest connection with the great reaction and restoration in the political field following the storms of that revolution and of Bonapartist rule in Europe. There is hardly a liberal school left now which dares openly profess that much-derided theory of a "social compact." This, I believe, is somewhat different in the United States. As far as my knowledge goes, this theory—that is to say, an individualistic construction of society and of the state—is still the ordinary method employed in this country for a deduction of the normal relations between state or society, on the one hand, and individuals, on the other; for, as needs no emphasis, it is not the opinion of an original contract in the historical sense that is to be held in any way as a substantial element of the theory. And yet the obvious criticism of that pseudo-element has been the most powerful argument against the whole theory, which consequently has seldom met with an intelligent and just appreciation in these latter days. And it is in opposition to it that, apart from a revival of theological interpretations, the recent doctrine of society or state as an organism has become so popular for a time.

This doctrine, of course, was an old one. Not to speak of the ancients, in the so-called Middle Ages it has preceded the contract theory, as it has supplemented it in more modern times. It was, indeed, coupled with the theological conceptions and religious ideals so universally accepted in those days although it was not dependent upon them. The doctrine of St. Thomas [Aquinas] and of Dante, however, contains a theory of the universal state; that is to say, of the empire, not a theory of society, of which the conception had not yet been formed, as we may safely say that a consciousness of it did not exist. This traditional organicism—applied as well to the Church, the mystic body, of which Christ was the supposed head —has been transferred of late to "society," after it had regained fresh authority as a political doctrine. However, the conception of a "society," as distinguished from political or religious bodies, is much more vague and indefinite. Either it is to be taken in the first and second sense, which I have pointed out as a biological or a psychological aspect of collective life, in which case organic analogies hold, but the whole consideration is not properly sociological; or it may be taken in our third, or sociological, sense, in which case it implies much less than any corporation the idea of what may be called an organization. It is well known that a lively controversy has been aroused about the new organicist theory, as proposed by Mr. Spencer and others, chiefly among those sociologists who center in the Institut International of Paris, where the late lamented M. Tarde played so prominent a part. Tarde has been among the foremost combatants against the vague analogies of organicism; and I fully agree with most of his arguments as set forth in the third sociological congress of 1897. I even flatter myself on having anticipated some of them in an early paper of mine upon Mr. Spencer's sociological work; which paper, however, did not become known beyond the small public of the *Philosophische Monatshefte* (1888). I have especially, and to a greater degree than Tarde, insisted upon the radical difference between a physiological division of labor and that division which is a cardinal phenomenon of society. I said: If we justly call it a division of labor that England manufactures cotton and China produces tea, and that the two countries exchange their products, then there is not and has not been a common labor or function preceding this division and dividing itself, as in the case of an organism; no state of society being historically known where China and England were one whole, working in harmony upon the spinning wheel and upon the tea plant. This is far from being true; each had its own historical development until they met in the mutual want of barter; and even this consideration implies that the countries themselves may justly be said to entertain trade and commerce with each other, though this is hardly more than a *façon de parler* with respect to a country like China.

It may be objected that there is a better analogy if we think of a primitive household, where labor is indeed one and is shifting among members of the community, while at a later stage it splits up into several families, some cultivating the soil, some becoming warriors or priests or artisans and tradesmen. And in the same way a village community, even an independent township like the ancient or medieval city, and a whole territory of which a city is the center, may reasonably be conceived of as one real household, of which all single households form organic parts. They would thus be contrasted with modern society, which is more adequately conceived of as a mere aggregate of individual households, each pursuing its own interest, maybe at the cost of all the others. This is my own objection, and this view is contained in my own theory of *Gemeinschaft* and *Gesellschaft,* meaning the dualism of that primitive economic condition surviving in many respects down to our own days, on the one hand, and commercial or capitalistic society, of which the germs are traceable in any form of what, with an abstract term, may be called communism, on the other. It is the former sense that even modern political economy may be spoken of (as we style it in German) as "national" economy. But even if this be allowed, the organic analogy does not hold other than in a rather indefinite way. Where is the one "social body" which thus evolves its organs and members, being in its early stage like a single household or a village community, and growing to be a complex *ensemble* of manors and municipalities and great cities, some of which have their manufactures working for foreign export, some for inland consumption? Is it England that has taken a development of this kind? Or is it England and Wales? Or are Scotland and even poor conquered Ireland to be included?

The more we should try to follow out the admirable attempt which Herbert Spencer has made in this direction of employing the organicist view as a working hypothesis, the more we should become convinced that our real insight into the lines along which social evolution travels is more hampered than promoted by that method of biological analogies.

III

But did I not say there was truth in the biological conception of social life? Indeed I did, and I say so again, if social life is considered externally and if we speak of a group as a living whole, where life is understood in its genuine sense, that is to say, biologically. And from this point of view, as that famous term, "physiological division of labor," is borrowed from economic fact and theory, we may, vice versa, apply physiological terms to social life considered externally. We may speak of organs and functions in a nation or society, or even with respect to mankind at large. We may metaphorically call the civilized nations the "brain" of humanity, and we may say that the United States has become an independent lobe of the cortex in the course of the last forty years. In the same way it was only lately, I understand, that your President spoke of railways as the arteries through which the blood of trade is circulating. The force of this metaphor will, I believe, not be impaired by the fact that several theorists point in more than a figurative sense to money or credit as the social fluid into which all substances of commodities are changed and which nourishes again the social brain and social muscles; that is to say, men and women who perform mental and physical work; in consequence of which analogy banks, and their correspondence by letters and bills and checks, would, more than railways, resemble arteries and veins. Of course, it would be small trouble to adduce a number of similar ambiguities, which make sociological inquiries of this kind appear as a matter of rhetoric and poetry but not of science.

Is there no other, no philosophical, truth at least in the comparison of a corporation to a living body? If there is, it can, according to the present view, be only in this respect, that a corporation may be thought and felt as an organic whole, upon which the members think and feel themselves dependent in such a way that they consider their own individual existence as subservient to the life of the whole. The question whether a society *is* an organism must be kept apart from the question whether there are societies the relations of which to their members are so qualified as to imply thoughts and feelings of that kind on the part of their members. We are well aware that social systems, which have been called by some eminent authors "ancient society," truly exhibited this characteristic trait. Why is not modern society—and, above all, the modern state—an organism in this peculiar sense?

I believe, indeed, that there is strong reason for controverting the theory in its application to these collective beings as they actually are. We live, as everybody knows, in an individualistic age, and we seek each other's company, chiefly for the benefit that accrues from it; that is to say, in a comparatively small degree from motives of sentiment and to a comparatively great extent from conscious reflection. It is this which makes us regard the state also as an instrument fit for serving our particular interests or those we have in common with some or with all of our fellow citizens rather than as an organism, ideally preexistent to ourselves, living its own life, and being entitled to sacrifices of our life and property in its behalf. It is true that in extraordinary times we live up to this view, but then we do not speak so much of society and of the state as of the fatherland which puts forward its claim to what we call our patriotism. A feeling of brotherhood and fellowship, of which in ordinary times the traces are as sadly scarce among compatriots as among those who are strangers to each other, rises, in moments of

public danger, from the bottoms of our souls in effervescent bub-
bles. The feeling, to be sure, is more of the nature of an emotion
than of a lasting sentiment. Our normal relations toward our present societies and states must not be taken as being accommodated
to this extraordinary standard. They are, howsoever men may
boast of their patriotism, generally of a calm and calculating character. We look upon the state, represented as it is by its government, as upon a person who stands in contractual rather than in
sentimental relations to ourselves. Certainly this view is more or
less developed in different countries, under different circumstances,
with different individuals. But it is the one that is endorsed by
the most advanced and the most conscious members of modern
societies, by those powerful individuals who feel themselves as
masters of their own social relations. Societies and states are chiefly
institutions for the peaceful acquisition, and for the protection, of
property. It is therefore the owners of property to whom we must
look when we are inquiring into the prevailing and growing conceptions of society and of the state. Now it cannot be doubted that
they do not consider either society or the state as representing that
early community which has always been supposed to be the original proprietor of the soil and of all its treasures, since this would
imply that their own private property had only a derivative right
—derived from the right and law of public property. It is just the
opposite which they think and feel: the state has a derivative right
of property by their allowance and their contributions; the state
is supposed to act as their mandatary. And it is this view which
corresponds to the facts. A modern state—it is by no means always
the youngest states that are the most characteristic types of it—
has little or no power over property.

I cannot refrain from quoting here, as I have done elsewhere, a
few sentences of the eminent American sociologist Lewis Morgan,
in which he sums up his reflections upon modern as contrasted
with ancient society. "Since the advent of civilization the out-
growth of property has been so immense, its forms so diversified,
its uses so expanding, and its management so intelligent in the
interests of its owners, that it has become, on the part of the people,
an unmanageable power. The human mind stands bewildered in

the presence of its own creation." He thinks it is true that "the time will come when human *intelligence* will rise to the mastery over property, and will be able to *define* the relations of the state to the property it protects, as well as the obligations and the limits of the rights of its owners." He declares himself unwilling to accept "a mere property career" as the final destiny of mankind.

But this outlook into a future far distant—although it was written, I believe, before there were any of the giant trusts established and before anybody in these states seemed to realize the dangers of the enormous power of combined capital—does not touch immediately the present question. It is the actual and real relation of the state to individuals which best reflects itself in the lack of power over property, as pointed out by Mr. Morgan, or, in other words, in the subservient position which the governments hold, in all countries more or less, toward the wealth-possessing classes. I do not say—although maybe I think—that this ought to be different; *"je ne propose rien, j' expose."* It is merely as a theoretical question that I touch upon this point. But I am not prepared to deny that it is also the great practical problem of social structure to reconstruct the state upon a new and enlarged foundation; that is to say, to make it, by common and natural effort, a real and independent being, an end in itself, a common wealth (in two words) administered not so much for the benefit of either a minority or a majority, or even of the whole number of its citizens, as for its own perpetual interests, which should include the interests of an indefinite number of future generations—the interests of the race. It cannot be overlooked that there are at present many tendencies at work in this direction, but I believe they are in part more apparent than real. The problem, we should confess, is an overwhelming one; and I for one do not feel at all sure that this splendid and transcendent constitution of ours will overcome its difficulties; that there will be sufficient *moral* power even if intelligence should rise to a sufficient height for solving in a truly rational way the "social question" as a question of social structure.

To sum up the argument, I put it in the form of a few theses or propositions:

1. The object of sociological theory proper, in distinction from

either biological or psychological, though these be ever so closely connected with it, is the corporation, for the most part represented, as it is, by a constituted body.

2. Religious faith makes some of the most important corporations appear as real, organic, mystic, and even supernatural beings. Philosophical criticism is right in discovering and explaining that all are creations of man and that they have no existence except insofar as human intellect and human will are embodied in them.

3. But nominalism is not the last word of a scientific philosophy. The existence of a corporation is fictitious indeed, but still is sometimes more than nominal. The true criterion is whether it be *conceived* and felt as a mere tool or machine, without a life of its own, or as something organic, superior to its temporary members. The true nature, however, of this conception is legible only from facts.

4. As a matter of fact, modern society and the modern state are prevailingly of a nature to correspond to an individualistic and nominalistic conception and standpoint. This is distinctly perceptible in the relation of the public power to private property.

5. This relation, and the relation dependent upon it, may substantially change in the course of time. An organic commonwealth may spring into existence which, though not sanctioned by any religious idea, and not claiming any supernatural dignity, still, as a product of human reason and conscious will, may be considered to be real in a higher sense than those products, as long as they are conceived as mere instruments serving the interests and objects of private individuals.

8

THE DIVISIONS OF SOCIOLOGY

I DISTINGUISH, first of all, general and special sociology. General sociology is the generalized study of human living together. This comprises all relationships of men in space and time, independent of whether or not they know each other, or have any relationship to each other, or whether they have a full or limited knowledge, or no knowledge at all, of each other's existence, whether they accept or reject each other, whether they live in a primitive state (formerly called a state of nature), or whether they live together or against each other in a state of a more or less developed culture. The study includes *all* these very diversified forms. But it excludes all kinds of social engineering (*Kunstlehren*) related to any one of these relationships; it only wishes to be a science of what is; this includes, however, what was and what will be, to the extent that it may become knowable.

The entire complex can be approached more specifically, depending on whether (1) the biological or (2) the psychological aspects are considered and explored or, finally, (3) out of both of them a specifically sociological investigation emerges.

In this sense, social biology and social psychology have at-

Translated from "Einteilung der Soziologie," *Soziologische Studien und Kritiken* 2 (1926) : 431–42; first published in *Zeitschrift fuer die gesamte Staatswissenschaft*, vol. 79, book 1 (1925) and presented before the Fifth International Philosophical Congress in Naples, which took place 5–9 May 1924. This paper, known as the "Naples paper," may be considered as the principal systematic forerunner of the book-length *Introduction to Sociology* (1931).

tained a position which includes them into general sociology, from which, however, special sociology is to be strictly distinguished.

General Sociology

Social biology, corresponding to its name, may also be extended to include the symbioses of plants and the so-called animal societies, but may be considered as a part of general sociology only to the extent that it explores human living together. In this sense, it also is called social anthropology. The subject of this science is man as an animal creature that feeds itself and procreates, moves back and forth and settles down, and, in the pursuance of all this, changes the surface of the earth, cultivates the soil, builds houses and ships, invents utensils, instruments and tools; all these things and the labor which produces them are of interest for this approach only inasmuch as they are *objective facts* which are part of the living together, that is, the very existence of man, furthering or hampering it. Likewise, the living together itself must be considered as far as it means mutual aid or, to the contrary, mutual damage and destruction in the world of external phenomena. The living together in space and time—that is, human life as a process of living next to each other, following each other, with and for or in spite and in defiance of each other—is here a sum total of natural events, which are subject to the general natural laws of growth and decay. These laws would be no less effective, if the living together were not accompanied, and even guided, by feelings and ideas. Within the area of social anthropology, psychology may thus be altogether disregarded.

Social anthropology deals with the races of mankind and their subdivisions insofar as their existence in large measure implies a spatial distribution of the human species continuing over long periods of time and a corresponding inbreeding; but also insofar as interbreeding with discernible results occurs and as consequently people of either the same or of different races and their subdivisions cooperate or are in a state of conflict with each other. To this area belong the questions of improvement and degeneration of the race together with the whole struggle for existence of naturally related human groups, struggles against the resistance of nature, struggles against each other for living space and for power and domination (*Herrschaft*). Power and domination may also be considered merely external facts, particularly the external coercion exerted by some against others for the purpose of making them serviceable and operating them like raw or processed objects of nature. Social biology is found as a component in several independently pursued sciences and can be singled out from these. *Ethnography* describes ethnic groups (*Voelker*), particularly primitive peoples whose culture is underdeveloped as far as the means of external existence are concerned. Next to ethnography may be placed demography, that is, the description of civilized nations, which provides insight into their life more thoroughly by means of enumeration and tabulation. Ethnography becomes ethnology, and demography becomes demology, that is, special sciences of the causal relationships between the phenomena observed. Ethnology and demology transfer their generalized results to social biology, which, in turn, transfers their elements to the theory of population; the descriptive sections, ethnography and demography, can be summarized as "sociography," which corresponds to the original and genuine meaning of statistics and is to be utilized in social biology, social psychology, and special sociology. Sociography also includes whatever belongs to the science of political economy, under the heading of "descriptive economics."

Social psychology is the necessary complement to social biology, as psychology generally complements biology. Social psychology considers all the factors included in the biological approach to human existence from the inner, psychic, or subjective side. It makes us perceive how people are brought together, kept together, and drawn close to each other by manifold motives, but also, on the other hand, how they are disunited, become hostile and alienated from each other by equally manifold motives. In these considerations men are conceived as individual carriers of a will, each of whom has particular psychic experiences in relation to all others and confirms or negates them to a lesser or larger degree. In addition, social psychology deals with those psychic experiences which are shared by several people inasmuch as they feel and react in the same way and want one and the same thing collectively. It is on account of this difference that Hans L. Stoltenberg has distinguished between "sociopsychology" and "psychosociology."

We accept this distinction and recognize in psychosociology the transition to the third division of general sociology, that is, to special sociology or sociology proper. The border area which, at the same time, is the first half of a bridge, includes the theory of social will, inasmuch as it is conceived as the common will of several individuals, but not yet as the unified will of an entity based on a common will, or a social entity.

Psychosociology thus includes the theory of masses (mass psychology) and of groups to the extent to which they are considered as merely externally connected aggregates.

Special Sociology

I subdivide special sociology into: *pure sociology; applied sociology; empirical sociology.* The reason for this subdivision is methodological; pure sociology is constructive, applied sociology is deductive, and empirical sociology is inductive.

Pure Sociology

Within pure sociology, I distinguish the following subdivisions: the basic concepts of *Gemeinschaft* and *Gesellschaft;* the theory of social entities; the theory of social norms, dealing with the content of the will of social entities; the theory of social values, dealing with the objects in the possession of social entities; the theory of social structures or institutions (*Bezugsgebilde*), dealing with the objects of action of social entities. These subdivisions are based on the concept of social entity. Social entity is conceived of as that which is not directly experienced; it must be seen and comprehended through the medium of the common thought and will of those individuals who are part of such an entity and who designate it. Such an entity exists only by means of this common will and therefore must always be conceived of as dependent on it. But the place of individuals or natural persons can also be taken by corporations or fictitious persons.

Basic concepts of sociology. The theory of the common will and its forms is the last extension of psychosociology, and consequently belongs to the area of social psychology, but leads from there directly to pure sociology. Within pure sociology, right at the entrance to it, I put the concepts of *Gemeinschaft* and *Gesellschaft*. The meaning of these concepts is that all relations among people as well as the derived relations of social corporations with individuals and with each other, even the relations between men and their gods, which like social entities are products of their imagination—all these complexes of positive relations which constitute a bond among men—(*vinculum*) have a twofold origin: either man's essential will or his arbitrary will. I conceive here as essential will the forms of volition, that is, affirmation as well as negation, which have their roots in feeling (in natural inclination and in instinct). They are strengthened by exercise or by way of habit and fulfilled as belief or trust. Part of essential will is also the affirmative volition inasfar as it is a means to an end, but only as long as these means are experienced and conceived in essential unity with the purpose. At this point, however, the break occurs, if and inasmuch as end and means fall apart, that is, if and when a means, in total isolation, finally indeed in opposition to the purpose, nevertheless is affirmed and willed as expedient; this occurs even in spite of an aversion which must be overcome, for instance, resistance, disgust, or remorse. The unit of *these* forms of willing I call arbitrary will. I understand community (*Gemeinschaft*) as based on essential will, association (*Gesellschaft*) as based on arbitrary will. Throughout, these concepts are logical, not genetic, in character.

The theory of the types of social entities. Among social entities, I distinguish: social relations, social collectives, and social corporations.

A social relation is essentially different from a natural as well as a psychological relation among men.

The *natural* relation among men, first of all, is an object of biological knowledge, therefore also of social biology. Individuals

of the human species are interrelated like the individuals of another species by the facts: (1) that one organism descends from
another, most directly from the mother organism; (2) that male and
female individuals need each other for the purpose of procreation
and therefore are attracted to each other; (3) that they are more
or less akin, therefore more or less similar to each other; so that
for these natural reasons they remain spatially close and have easy
contact with each other. Natural relations, therefore, differ widely,
according to their content, strength, and meaning. One may consider all people as brothers and sisters, but one will do so the more,
the closer they are related by descent; within such multitudes, one
may think of each generation as the mother of the following and
the daughter of the preceding generation. But this always would
have only a biological, not a psychological or sociological, meaning.

The *psychological* relation between people consists in the objective fact that they feel attracted to, or repelled by, each other
either (a) by inclination or disinclination, familiarity or strange-
ness, trust and a sense of obligation, or by mistrust and a sense of
antagonism, or (b) by self-interest, calculation of advantage,
awareness of the usefulness or harmfulness of the other for one's
own purposes: that is, either by essential will or by arbitrary will.
Consequently, one may say that people feel related to each other
by the fact that they think of each other as belonging together as
natural friends and comrades, or as hampering and excluding each
other, as real or possible—more or less probably—antagonists and
enemies. A psychological relation of the former kind may be conceived of as a positive, that of the latter kind as a negative relation.

A *social* relation evolves from a positive psychological relation
to the extent that it is not only experienced, thought of, and known
as such but also affirmed and willed as existing and permanent.
Every social relation is more or less based on a natural relation
inasmuch as this relation is, or becomes at the same time, a positive psychological relation. A good example is the archetype of a
communal relationship: the relation of mother and child. According to its origin as a natural relation, it is in the beginning a one-
sided psychological relation and as such not essentially different
from the relation to a beloved object. Normally, the one-sided rela-

tion becomes a mutual one and is affirmed as such by both subjects and consciously conceived as permanent and real. It is this consciousness that marks man as man. The Oedipus myth and the tragedy originating from it movingly express the dreadful fate which derives from ignorance and error in this regard.

By the will to continuity and permanency as well as by the consciousness of its correctness, the social relation connecting man and woman is raised to the status of marriage. The German word *Ehe* denotes—if perhaps not in its origin, so in its meaning—unlimited continuation, that is, eternity (*Ewigkeit*). Religious ideas and legal prohibitions usually protect this will to a legitimate marriage; but this protection is not an essential part of marriage as a social relation. Considered purely sociologically—without regard to legal validity or prevailing moral ideas—common-law marriage (*Gewissensehe*), too, is a real marriage if the mutual firm will to the relation, that is, enduring faithfulness, prevails and proves itself in it; such a marriage may even surpass the average of legally valid marriages in its quality as true marriage.

It belongs to the essence of every social relation as a mutual relationship approved by both parts that each of the persons involved makes and asserts a claim to a certain—regular or occasional, more or less permanent—conduct of the other person or persons; in other words, that conduct is expected as originating from their free will and conforming to the wish and will (the self-interest) of those who expect it. This mutual attitude is demanded and dictated by the common and uniform will essential to a social relation which appears as the will of the relationship itself, because the relationship is conceived in terms of an entity. It is therefore the relationship which generates duties or obligations, which raises corresponding demands and consequently also negates and prohibits free actions contradicting these obligations. In societal (*Gesellschaft*-like) relations, rights and obligations differ from each other with rational distinctness. We know of totalities of internally connected relations: such a relation is the family as the epitome of relations which are communal (*Gemeinschaft*-like) in their essence. Societal relations may also be connected in this manner and form an indeterminate unit: for instance, a number of people interested in the same business, as far as they know each other in this role.

We are here confronted with the transition to the second concept of a social entity, that is, the concept of the *collective*. By collective, I understand a number of individuals who are so connected with each other by natural or positive psychological or social relations between themselves that they are thought of as a unit. Natural collectives are those units of a biological character in which men of every age, both sexes, and any conceivable residence are comprised: as race, people, tribe, or other genealogical complexes to which the individuals belong and by which they are conditioned inasmuch as they have inherited from their ancestors the characteristics, or qualities, peculiar to such blood-related collective totalities. These collectives are psychic in nature, inasmuch as those qualities are psychic and manifest themselves in psychic phenomena. However, there also exist psychic collectives that are essentially determined not by natural but by psychic attributes, namely, by the abilities and achievements of its members. Such are linguistic and religious collectives, vocational groups, and the like, all of them considered quite externally as objective facts, as territorial census and statistical enumeration count them without thinking of drawing any conclusions regarding inner cohesion and social relationships. I call these and others *social* collectives if they are willed and affirmed by the people belonging to them more or less clearly and consciously and either emotionally or rationally: they are thus supported more by essential or more by arbitrary will and correspond either more to the category of *community* or more to the category of *association*. I subdivide social collectives into (1) those which are essentially economic and caused by economically determined social facts; (2) those which are essentially politically determined; (3) those which are essentially mentally and morally determined. Examples are: (1) Estates and classes; (2) the nation, civil society; (3) Christendom, the republic of letters, artistic or philosophical schools of thought, and so forth.

The social entity reaches fulfillment in the concept of the *corporation* and the social body. In this form, the concept is exclusively sociological: the social entity now is no longer conceived merely as such, but as a *person*, that is to say, it is conceived, like the gods, as a rational being; it thinks, consults, and decides; it has a will and asserts that will. Here we encounter *Gemeinschaften* and *Gesellschaften*, unions and associations of all kinds and, again: (1) in the economic, that is, the general social area; (2) in the political area; and (3) in the mental and moral area. The most important examples are, (1) the clan, the village community, the guild as communal (*Gemeinschaft*-like) bodies; the joint-stock companies, cartels and trusts as associational (*Gesellschaft*-like) bodies; (2) commonwealths (*Gemeinwesen*) and leagues (*Buende*) as communal groupings, states (in the modern sense) and political organizations as associational groupings; (3) religious communities, religious orders, churches according to the category of *Gemeinschaft*, and associations formed for religious or other moral purposes according to the category of *Gesellschaft*.

The essential and basic reason for the existence of social relations, collectives, and corporations is always the will of the natural or collective persons of which they are composed. In the second place, however, they gain existence through external recognition, which as such follows their formation, by other natural or collective persons; but such approval may also be the cause, that is, the condition, of their existence, which in this case appears as "made" and preceding the naturally evolving existence. But the actual life of social relationships rests exclusively with this natural existence which evolves through the wills of the participating individuals. Finally, every social entity attains a third form of existence, the quasi-objective one, in the mind of the observer and the thinker who both knows and acknowledges it.

Corporations in particular may also be established and organized by an exterior will, be it an individual will or a collective will. They are then subsumed under the general concept of the institution (*Anstalt*): they are founded. Collective will can establish the foundation either directly—by a resolution (a decree)—or indirectly: by a charter, that is, within the whole complex of a stipulation about the rules of cooperation in a social body.

The difference and the contrast of *Gemeinschaft* and *Gesellschaft* are also evident in social bodies. But these concepts in all their manifestations must be interpreted in such a way that transitions from one form to the other appear possible and under certain conditions probable.

The theory of social norms. The next and third area of pure sociology is the theory of social norms. Social norms are general precepts and prohibitions imposed by a social entity (relation, collective, or corporation) concerning the subjects or members, that is, primarily individuals, which is to say, all precepts restricting the freedom of their conduct and binding their will. They are of great variety and of very different extension and intensity. They restrict relations, collectives, and corporations as well as individuals.

I distinguish between: norms of order; norms of law; norms of morality.

The social forms of will on which norms as the contents of volition are based are:

The communal (*Gemeinschaft*-like) form of will, which I call: (a) concord (the totality of all common willing which because it is based on communal relationships seems to be self-evident as both natural and necessary); (b) custom (basis: communal habit); (c) religion (basis: the communal belief in supernatural ruling and norm-giving powers).

The societal (*Gesellschaft*-like) forms of will, which I call— (a) convention (the totality of all willing which is conceived as a means for common purposes, by expressed or tacit agreement); (b) legislation (a common will which demands a certain action or abstinence from action as necessary in the sense that a will to compel, to coerce, or to impose a punishment is connected with it); (c) public opinion (a common will which exercises critical judgment for the sake of a common interest and thereby affects "private" forms of conduct and action in either a restraining or furthering manner).

Order, law, and morality have been distinguished according to the following viewpoints. (1) Order is the most general complex of norms. It is based predominantly on concord or convention, more or less on either form of social volition. (2) Law is the complex of norms which according to their idea, that is, the will, on which they are based, are to be interpreted and applied by judicial verdict. This complex develops more or less through custom (common law) or through formal purposively conceived legislation (statute law). (3) Morality is a complex of norms, the interpretation and application of which is conceived as the competence of an ideal judge, be it a god or an abstract entity, reason, or conscience, or of mankind or any ideal entity; as, for instance, humanitarianism. These norms are formed and more or less confirmed either by religion or by public opinion. In both forms they react upon the general social and particularly the political domain.

All forms and contents of the social will are in a variety of ways interrelated and interwoven with each other. All social relations, collectives, and corporations exist, in the first place, in the first-named complex of norms: they have an orderly existence; secondarily, they have a legal existence; and, finally, a moral existence. One or the other kind of existence finds in them its stronger or weaker expression, depending upon their more communal or more associational character. It is the special task of the theory of social norms to describe and analyze this diversity.

The theory of social values. The fourth main section of pure sociology comprises the theory of social values. Social values are: the objects of social volition, (1) inasmuch as this willing aims at the objects themselves, confirms and appreciates them, wants to keep them, or acquires them; (2) inasmuch as it feels and knows itself in command of them, in other words, as it possesses them. The concept of social value reaches perfection in a more or less absolute desire to keep in possession, depending on the degree and kind of appreciation. I subdivide social values into:

(1) Economic values. To these belong all material objects in common possession. Human individuals are included, inasfar as they are conceived as such objects, be it as things, like slaves, or as persons, like children. I can merely mention here the significance of the social property of land and other immobilia but also of movable things and the problems connected with it; the values of mineral resources; and material values which at the same time have an ideal significance.

(2) Political values. These are partly material, partly ideal

values. To the former belong: the territory of a country or of a town, even though such territory may not be conceived of as common property; the means of defense and attack available to a political community, the houses of assembly, the instruments and documents of political life. Political values of ideal significance are partly the same, partly the institutions, constitutions, laws, and rights, inasmuch as the national community affirms them and wishes to preserve them, at least in their basic substance.

(3) Ideal and spiritual values. These are: (a) *persons* who are generally esteemed and honored; included are persons who are alive or have lived as well as persons who are imaginary, that is, men as well as gods, deified heroes, saints, and the like; (b) *objects,* such as works of art, of the performing as well as the visual arts, and also of science, which are felt and thought of as common property, in particular cases as national property. Common language, native customs and habits, religion in its specific cultural manifestations, all of these in their capacity as such goods or social values may be objects of passionate love and devotion; (c) the social signs—a very varied and significant group of ideal social values. The nature of a sign is not so much its material existence as its meaning and validity. Its value consists precisely in its validity.

I subdivide social signs into:

(a) Signs standing for social values. To these belongs language as a system of signs for the ideal value of mutual understanding and the capability to communicate; further, writing, including printing, as a sign of signs. Finally, all the so-called value symbols are included here, the most important of which is money: as symbols of material values they belong to these, quite aside from the fact that at the same time they *are* material values—like hard cash or *specie.*

(b) Purposive signs, for the will that something should be or should be done. They are differentiated according to the norms which indicate what ought to be. Consequently, we have signs of valid order, valid law, valid morality; these include signals— agreed upon or imposed, acoustic or optic—as well as judicial decrees and laws, for which particular forms and formalities are signs of their legal validity; finally, there are corresponding signs for morally valid concepts and rules.

(c) Symbols. These are signs expressed in words, actions, or objects, denoting in a more specific sense relations, situations, or norms which are understood either as existing, that is, having validity, or as desirable, that is, signs which ought to have validity. Signs, like ideally conceived values generally, can be determined and conditioned to a larger or lesser degree by essential or by arbitrary will; their meaning, to a larger or lesser degree, can be communal or associational.

The theory of social structures or institutions (*Bezugsgebilde*). As the fifth and last area of pure sociology, I describe social structures, or institutions, that is, the systems of activities in which the social will of every kind is manifested. Such structures, or institutions, have: (a) economic, (b) political, (c) spiritual-moral character. Subdivisions are: (a) domestic economy, city economy, regional economy, national economy, world economy; (b) all kinds of human communities (commonwealths), legal systems, defense systems, constitutions; (c) all systems of religion, the arts, philosophy, the sciences, instruction, and education.

All social structures, or institutions (*Bezugsgebilde*) may also be conceived of as social values, and several already were mentioned as such above. But in the present context they have a different meaning: that of parts of a living culture which is being fostered and promoted or inhibited and corrupted and whose state conditions and keeps dependent all other manifestations of social life, that is, all other objects of pure sociology.[1]

---

[1]   The last two sections of this paper, dealing with the divisions of applied and empirical sociology, are omitted. Formulations comparable to those contained in these sections may be found in the following chapters in this volume: "Social Structures or Institutions: Effectiveness of Factors"; "Statistics and Sociography"; "The Individual and the World in the Modern Age."—EDS.

III. Pure Sociology

Editors' note. *In his book* Einfuehrung in die Soziologie[1] *Toennies deals only with special sociology and, here again, only with pure sociology. He omits what he designates as general sociology, that is, physical anthropology, demography and social psychology, and within special sociology he presents only the sketchiest outline of applied and empirical sociology. He considers statements in pure sociology as conceptual, that is, as static rather than dynamic in character although he cannot help introducing a dynamic element whenever he refers to concrete examples to illustrate a concept. The entire work is divided into six "books." The first book defines essential and arbitrary will as well as* Gemeinschaft *and* Gesellschaft *as basic concepts. The second book deals with social entities or configurations, namely, social relations, collectives, and corporations. The third book deals with social values, namely, economic, political, and ethical values. The fourth book deals with social norms, namely, order, law, and morality. The fifth book deals with social structures or institutions and its principal "factors," namely economics, politics, and spirit (= Geist = culture in a narrower sense). The sixth book, which has the character of an appendix, outlines the fields of applied (= historical) and empirical sociology.*

The excerpts are from books II, III, IV, and V.

[1]   1st ed., 1931. Chapters 9–15, this volume, are translated from the 2d ed. (Stuttgart: Ferdinand Enke, 1965).

9

SOCIAL ENTITIES OR

CONFIGURATIONS:

GENERAL CHARACTERIZATION

Social Relations and Social Collectives

PURE SOCIOLOGY, in the first place, is the theory of social entities or configurations. The concepts of social entities are presented most perfectly through corporations, that is, through associations which signify for the consciousness of their own members a unit capable of willing and acting, in other words, a person comparable to an individual human being. However, I distinguish separately from these as conceptual steps: (1) social relations, (2) social collectives. Both are to be conceived as basically similar to corporations, namely, insofar as they move, influence, determine, and, in an extreme case, force individual wills.

Social relations in their simplest form are dualistic, but they can be extended and, as a unit of several pair relationships, become a social circle. Relations exist through a common will of two or more persons to give each other mutual aid or other support, the least that can be done being mutual toleration or refraining from hostility. But for their carriers or subjects they are not units capable of will or action. I relate all kinds of social relations to the rational and ideal type of "alliance," especially because this concept is mainly applied to relations between such important corporations as states; for states, or governments, are the most extreme types of social configurations which, as persons capable of willing and acting, are, and ought to be, controlled exclusively through arbitrary will, and therefore represent the essence of the

Translated from *Einfuehrung in die Soziologie*, book 2, chap. 1, pp. 19–34 (§5). Subheadings are adapted from the table of contents.

egotistical volition in pure type. This type can serve as the measure
for all kinds of relationships.

Alliance As a Rational and Ideal Type of Social Relations

The alliance—whether between natural or artificial (fictitious) persons—is concluded by means of a contract, that is,
through an agreement of wills, principally of two such persons.
This agreement has a definite purpose which always implies mutual
aid. Immanent in the alliance is the tendency toward unified action
which, in cases where the alliance is one between states, becomes
evident in times of war as common attack or common defense.

A contract, or treaty, presupposes the formal equality of the
contracting persons, insofar as they acknowledge or respect one
another, as in the same manner capable of being useful or harmful to each other, although possibly in varying degree. It always
implies a mutual promise which, reduced to its rational core, is
nothing but a statement about future action or the lack of it; one
as much as the other is meant by this statement to be made probable to a higher degree than would otherwise be the case. The will
thereby expressed with reference to future action or the lack of
it may be a more or less determined will; the opponent, that is, the
contracting party to whom a promise is made, receives and inter-
prets the statement as the sign of a more or less determined will,
that is, he deems the first to be bound by his declaration of intention; this means that he may be inclined to act in accordance with
the promise, both through his own determined will and through
the will of him to whom the promise was made: such conduct is
thus made doubly probable, insofar as the willing of two persons
is twice as probable as the willing of one.

The formal equality of the parties to the contract (*Paziszen-
ten*) signifies equal liberty of decision prior to the contract. If
this condition is fulfilled completely, both parties will be equally
bound by the alliance. In reality, this condition can never be fulfilled to perfection.

Social relations, as rationally (typically) represented by the alliance, exist in various shapes; some of these are not based on contracts at all or, if they are, spring more from essential than from arbitrary will. As naturally grown relations, those based on essential will are recognizable more easily in natural than in artificial persons. They are based mainly on natural—biological—relationships between human beings because of which human beings (not unlike many species of other living creatures) are driven toward mutual aid, be it through mutual attraction (sex drive, love, maternal and paternal instinct, pleasure in playing and living together) or through habit or through the sentiment and the thought of moral necessity or duty. This sentiment derives from habit or liking while thought changes into a growing awareness of self-interest, thus representing the transition toward a relationship based on arbitrary will.

Social relations of the kind mentioned—*Gemeinschaft*-like relations—do not presuppose formal equality or equal liberty of the persons involved; rather, they exist in part because of natural inequalities—of sex, age, physical, and moral forces within the actual conditions of life. But in part, they approach the ideal or rational type of alliance through equality or sufficient similarity of these conditions of life, such as sameness of sex, approximate sameness of age, similarity of physical and moral powers expressed in temperament, character, and especially in the way of thinking. But in these cases, too, mutual attraction, habituation, and the consciousness of mutual obligation are the psychological prerequisites of such social relationships. These, therefore, usually have their origin in the feeling and consciousness of interdependence, on account of kinship, spatial, or other common conditions of life: good and evil, hopes and fears. I perceive this fact in verbal form as being together (*Zusammenwesen*); the special phenomena evolving from proximity, as dwelling together (*Zusammenwohnen*); finally, those deriving chiefly from common conditions of life, as acting together (*Zusammenwirken*). Here the transition toward the rational configuration of the alliance is clearly evident. But this acting together (*Zusammenwirken*) is also the basis and form of the most spiritual relationship which may be understood as friendship, just as being together (*Zusammenwesen*) may be understood as blood relationship, and dwelling together (*Zusammenwohnen*) as neighborliness.

Social Collectives

All those phenomena which I will designate as collectives (*Samtschaften*) may be referred to the concept of "party" as ideal type. Party is here understood as the group one joins, the object one seizes, the viewpoint one chooses—all this insofar as it is done in the realization that it may be of advantage for one's own ends. Consequently, the party or "side" is a collective based on arbitrary will which is consciously "joined" ("taken") as a means for achieving more or less definite ends. It is a concept to which reality rarely corresponds perfectly. But it approaches it more nearly than other concepts of collectives in which the individual may find himself, and where he realizes far less that he has chosen such collectives of his own free will and for the purpose of furthering his own interests than is the case with regard to the party. Surely, one is justified in thinking of the party, especially the political party, that it is embraced or joined in this spirit. Indeed, as a rule, the advantages expected from the existence and the activities of a party are the motivation by the strength of which the party is formed and held together. That is so, even if often a strong conviction is upheld that the party's aims represent the absolute good and just and that the party holds a monopoly on truth. The subconscious and the conscious are often intermingled; and that which is explainable only through subjective attitudes strengthened by habit, tradition, and indoctrination appears as the plain truth, self-evident and of itself necessary. This is valid for the party's way of thinking, its prejudices and principles, and implicitly for the party itself and for one's adherence to it. In this regard, all collectives are similar to the party, insofar as their members approve of them, affirm them, and regard them to be of value.

In the same way in which every party finds itself in opposition to other parties, often hardening into open and bitter enmity, every other collective to a larger or lesser degree is aware of being the negation of one or several other similar collectives, of which one may surmise or know that their members have a comparable awareness and self-confidence. In this sense, the self-consciousness of a social estate (*Stand*) asserts itself against the self-consciousness of another estate, or estates, the self-consciousness of a social class against the self-consciousness of another class, or classes. The same is true of the self-consciousness of the common folk against the ruling class and vice versa, and the self-consciousness of an entire people against another people, or peoples. In this sense especially the "nation" has come about as a collectivity, confronting other nations in exclusion, negation, and even challenge, so that all this is regarded as the hallmark of a proper sense of nationality, a true national consciousness. "Nationality" asserts itself even more sharply against another or several other nationalities if, against its own will, it is politically tied to such a superordinated nationality. In all these cases and in many others—we may remember the relations of religious persuasions toward one another—the collective is a party or shows the tendency of becoming a party; but as a rule, it is far removed from the ideal type of party established here, which may be chosen by the arbitrary will as a tool for its own ends.

However, these collectives are more likely to be formed in combination with deep-seated feelings, such as love for one's kind, for one's native country, for one's language and customs, pride in one's ancestors, in possessions, especially in landed property and wealth. But it may also be combined with sentiments which spring from the lack of such privileges and goods, and these again may develop feelings of solidarity and comradeship, perhaps focused and expressed in a common love and admiration of the leader of a party, a common faith, and a common hope. It is natural for faith to be faith in the validity of one's own cause, the correctness, even sanctity, of one's own opinions, the justification, even necessity, of one's own striving. Religious faith in one's own god or gods, in their protection and aid, especially in battle, is only the elevated and transfigured expression of that personal faith. Hope is as natural and general as the faith of a party or another collective: the hope of every fighter for victory, that is, the hope to defeat his enemies and the pleasant consequences ensuing therefrom, be they the enjoyment of triumph or purely material advantages. Here, then, the approximation to the ideal type of the party described above becomes apparent, that is, when opposition between parties or collectives of some kind develops into conflict or war: the party is embraced because, by so doing, advantages are presumed to be gained. This happens in spite of complete indifference as to the value of the object, that is, the case of the conflict. For example, people without any political conviction, without even any consideration of interests of estate or class which might be concealed behind apparently independent convictions, join a party only because they expect it to be victorious and, knowing that the spoils belong to the victor, hope to snatch some of them. The same applies in wars between nations and states, if an initially neutral state decides, after a period of waiting, to support the country with the best chances to be the winner.

Social Corporations

The concept of association (*Verein*) represents most clearly the rational and ideal type of all organized groups (*Verbaende*) or social corporations (*Koerperschaften*) insofar as they are autogenous, meaning that they exist through the will of their members. For this concept the specific purpose which the association is meant to serve is not an essential element: only the form is relevant. We conceive of an association as coming into being through the combined wills of several individuals who meet for the purpose of initiating this association. They are unanimous in this will, therefore also in the will to establish a constitution, a system of rules for the association. Consequently, they regard the consensus of a section of the assembled as the expression of the will of all and let it be valid as such. Those assembled consider themselves as forming a unit for this purpose, as "an assembly competent to pass valid resolutions." The form by which the competence is achieved is the majority principle which results from simple, practical considerations.

Similarly, the typical constitution of an association comes into being. Provided there is a quorum, the membership meeting is established as the organ of the association, representing the will of all members. With this meeting rest the decisions about the affairs of the association, its will is considered to be the will of the association; the meeting is "sovereign," insofar as it intends and believes to be determined exclusively by its own will. But the membership meeting is only of ideal duration; its artificial body cannot remain assembled uninterruptedly in one place; its members disperse for shorter or longer periods. Thus it cannot easily and efficiently conduct the business of an association, because this requires a persevering and constant will. This task is normally transferred to a single person or to a small standing committee that can get together without difficulty: the board of directors of the association. Within this board, usually one single person or several persons in turn take the chair, that is, are in charge of the proceedings as required by the regulations for each meeting and for each committee. If the general meeting reserves final decisions to itself, it thereby restricts the powers of the board from the start and makes it "responsible" for carrying out the decisions that have been taken. But it is also conceivable that an association is founded by a narrow circle that can meet relatively easily, reserving all decisions for itself and creating an extended circle of members only to entitle them as individuals to share in the purposes and privileges of the association, without allowing the whole body to be an organ of the association. Even a single individual, a natural person, could, in this sense, gather around him a group of other persons who under him—the "head"—assist or offer him their services, just as he does to them, without their acquiring thereby any corporative competence of will and action. But in that case, the form of an association would be completely abolished; nevertheless, the group thus formed could be effective in the manner of a corporation, whose will would then be represented by the head, that is, a single natural person or persons; likewise where a small circle of people forms the association, the will of all, including the associate members, is represented through a small executive committee. In these two cases, however, a corporation can live only if and as long as its passive members recognize the permanent representation of their will and of the interests they have invested in the corporation, in the executive committee, or in the individual head.

Viewed from the abstract scheme of the association, this agreement of the passive members—who may constitute the large majority—may be thought of as a voluntary surrender of all activity and the transfer of the representation of their interests to the executive committee or to the head. Such a transfer can also be thought of and exist in extensive and highly important areas in such a way that the members of an association transfer to a smaller body the determination and the decision concerning common affairs but reserve for themselves the right to regulate the composition of this body through their own will; whether they elect members of this small corporation in smaller subdivisions or elect them at large. They might even reserve the right, in certain circumstances, to have a voice as a unit—after the constituent original assembly—in order to repeal decisions of the small corporation and perhaps also to alter regulations about its composition. It follows that the constitution of the association may contain, apart from such regulations about the powers of a small corporation—whether they include the final decision in every case or not—further rules about other powers of other corporations founded for the purposes of the association or of individual natural persons, each of whom has conferred upon himself, in accordance with such rules, duties which he is supposed to discharge in the name of the association.

If we take the abstract scheme of the formation of an association as the yardstick for all original autogenous corporations, we will soon notice that the more the corporation bears a *Gemeinschaft*-like character, the more remote from this scheme are their formation and their structure. This *Gemeinschaft*-like, or communal, character is either authoritarian (*herrschaftlich*), or cooperative (*genossenschaftlich*), or a combination of both types. In each case, it can be structured in such a way that its forms resemble the variation of the rational scheme which was distinguished from the normal scheme, because there is a passive membership who believe their will to be contained in the will of a single person or of a corporative group of active members. But the reason for the cohesion of a *Gemeinschaft*-like corporation, the motivating element of its union, is essentially different: it exists *before* the individuals and their purposes, not as in the ideal type of association (*Gesell-*

schaft), *after* the individuals and their purposes, and arising only from their getting together. It is based on essential will, not on arbitrary will. Therefore, the members of a *Gemeinschaft*-like union are persons who feel and know that they belong together on the ground of the natural closeness of their minds. This closeness may be temporal, namely that of descent, kinship or blood, or spatial, namely that of the place in which they live, be it a house, a home town, or an entire country, or, finally, the spiritual closeness of a communal way of thinking, namely that of a common and unifying faith, common desire, volition, and hope, all of which lead to a common reverence for human beings and gods, alive or dead. Of this kind are organized groups (*Verbaende*) in the field of religion or any other common persuasion and all such groups based on being, dwelling, or acting (working) together or on several or all three of these; consequently, they have a share in the essence of spiritual closeness, in other words, in a common way of thinking.

Authoritarian corporations are further removed from the type of the association than cooperative or egalitarian corporations. Authoritarian corporations may be based solely on the power of one or a few natural persons who look upon and treat all other persons who belong to the association as their slaves, servants, or subjects; and *these* may regard themselves as such and be kept only through fear in a kind of union with their master or masters, held together with one another by means of this common fear and the antagonism arising from it. In this case, an organized group, or corporation, corresponding to the sociological concept which has been employed here does not exist: for the meaning of our concept requires the affimation of the corporation by its members. Such affirmation is given only if the subjects or subordinates regard and acknowledge the authority (1) as natural, that is motivated by actual and necessary circumstances, in particular by natural conditions, as grounds for the social conditions, in other words as justified. For this, there are two normal, or ideal, types: (a) the familial: the image of the ruler is that of a father whom his children love and honor, to whom they owe nourishment and protection— and are also willing to reciprocate—whose anger they fear, finding his chastisements and punishments as well as his rewards and beneficent deeds just; (b) the religious form, that is, an imitation of the patriarchal or matriarchal authority. If all, masters and subjects, approach the throne of the Highest Being like children and servants; if they look up to God—the only one or the highest—as to a father, then there will spring from the imagined superiority of the Invisible a consecration and sanctification of the dominion of the visible overlord; the worldly authority will be supported and elevated through the supernatural authority.

(2) The other condition for an authoritarian corporation to continue in its existence, in spite of distance and difference between rulers and ruled, is that the ruled are not too dissatisfied with their condition and that they regard their state of satisfaction or even happiness, their prosperity and progress, to be due, in correspondence to the favor and grace of their invisible masters—the gods—to the favor and grace of their visible masters, who may even be thought of as appointed and protected by the invisible ones.

A cooperative corporation, too, differs from an association, unless it is different only by name, through its communal (*Gemeinschaft*-like) character, and perhaps also because of a communal origin. Its prototype is the brotherhood which is held together because of common parents, forefathers, ancestors, or which at least believes that it can trace itself and that which is its common heritage to these, and ultimately even to a mythical progenitor, if not a god. As a fellowship of worship (*Kultgenossenschaft*), even an authoritarian corporation may represent a brotherhood. Most likely, however, a brotherhood is based on common action, whether in combat—comradeship—or in peaceful cooperation. Neither its familial nor its religious foundation is of such special significance here as it is for the authoritarian corporation. Yet the authority which a group claims over individuals, the corporation over its members, can develop into domination by single natural persons or by one individual over the rest. Thus, once again, the kind of dominion arises that requires natural or supernatural confirmation —or both.

Both authoritarian as well as cooperative corporations differ from associations above all because of the universality of their character. Associations are intended and meant to be only means to

certain specific ends for their subjects, they are in their whole structure *Gesellschaft*-like, whereas authoritarian and cooperative corporations, unless they have become alienated from their origin or
from their original authenticity, belong to the type of *Gemeinschaft*
and are essentially based on it.

It is one thing if the concept of a spiritual or secular commonwealth (*Gemeinwesen*) is referred to the ideal type of an association (*Verein*) in such a way as we have done, something else
again if the same concept is subordinated to the general or generic
concept of association. To the strictly rational way of thinking
which dominated scientific thought about social relations and associations from Thomas Hobbes to Kant and Fichte and their successors, such a subordination seemed to be absolutely necessary.
This individualistic approach manifests itself in its purest form
in the dualistic construction: on the one hand, of a natural state of
man, a state of perfect freedom and anarchy; on the other hand of a
civil and political state which in logical consequence is conceived by
certain theories as one of ideal perfection: a perfect order is established and maintained therein through a common will, that is, the
will of all concentrated in the will of a single natural or fictitious
person. Between these two lies the agreement of the many, which
as a rule is conceived and designated as the social contract, as was
still clearly the case with Kant; for Hobbes, the agreement—according to the last form of his system—consists at first only in the
formation of an assembly, that is, in the tacit or expressed understanding that this assembly is to create the constitution of the association which is to be established, namely the state, by means of its
permanent competence in arriving at binding decisions until the
task is completed. The quintessence of this competence is that
agreement or disagreement with a suggested statute by the majority of the members of the assembly is considered to be the pronounced collective will of the entire assembly and is made apparent
as such. Whether the members of the assembly ever announce their
own will, in their own name or at the same time in the name of a
multitude that has given them the commission to do so, is not essential for the concept. But it must be presupposed that the totality
of the individuals who, as it were, want to make peace with one an-

other be "represented" by these members of the assembly. The constituent assembly has complete freedom to decide by majority vote as to which form of constitution it decides to adopt, unless all its members have received and accepted the binding mandate to decide in favor only of one particular form of constitution or to dissolve.

In the historic reality of recent centuries a tendency has become apparent which may be called a tendency toward the realization of the conceptual image. Only seemingly, at least only to a small degree, has the image itself contributed to this. That realization has gained momentum only when the image already was about to fade and when other less clear and logically less well-thought-out theorems had competed with it or even replaced it. Far more than under the influence of the theory of natural law, that realization has been gained under the influence of the general social development which is inadequately interpreted as the development of individualism. Individualism is the precondition of the new social structure, of the change in social relations, social collectives, and social corporations, of their constitution as *Gesellschaft*-like rather than as *Gemeinschaft*-like relationships, collectives, and corporations. Especially, individualism is the precondition for the most comprehensive political corporation, namely, the state. The significance of the state rests with the fact that it is the expression of the thought that the associational society (*Gesellschaft*), or the collective of the individuals living together in exchange and trade and a variety of contractually based relationships and corporations, requires a permanent bearer of authority and common will in order to settle controversies which may arise within it, to restrain them, if necessary, by force, to allay self-defense and other ways of taking the law into one's own hands, and to pursue common ends through common means; in particular, in external relations, a common force must be set up to counter any force which one has been subjected to or which is threatening.

Theoretical criticism has asserted with much emphasis and with considerable success: (1) that the actual origin of political commonwealths has been of a different kind; it has been stated that it was untrue that the state had developed through contracts or assemblies of individuals or representatives of these individuals; (2) that the essence of the state was not correctly designated by such a concept; to understand the state as a mere means toward the common ends of individuals would be a mechanical approach and therefore unworthy of it. The state, in the words of Georg Waitz, grows organically, as an organism; not, it is admitted, as a natural but as an ethical organism. This theory derives from Schelling's philosophy, which—more than any other in the German language area and elsewhere—has emphasized the irrational nature of life and of living beings and, following Spinoza's great conception, has focused philosophical thinking on it; this was before Schelling got lost in mysticism and theosophy. Sociologically, an ethical or social organism can be spoken of only insofar as its existence is placed into the minds of human beings who consider themselves to be the members or cells, or in their groups as the web of such an organism, or in certain functions or services which transcend individuals, as the organs of such an organism. I prefer to call the corporation whose general nature is described as that of the state a commonwealth (*Gemeinwesen*). Opposed to this meaning, to be sure, is the concept of the state as a mechanism, in its perfection even as a highly competent machine. Yet this concept is not an error or an incorrect point of view by some theoreticians; rather, it is self-constitutive, partly because it has grown out of one or several commonwealths, partly because it arises from special and new needs as a means to their ends. That is the "modern" state— the only possible conceptualization of a commonwealth which maintains itself on the assumption of isolated rational individuals who exchange goods and make contracts with one another; it maintains itself in concrete manifestations, such as laws, institutions, and the like. In reality, this perfect state, conceived as a societal (*Gesellschaft*-like) machine has not yet reached its completion in any country, and will perhaps never be completed anywhere. But all modern states tend to approach the ideal type, even though in different ways.

The closest approach to this form has occurred in colonial countries, because they enjoy greater freedom from traditionalism. "In colonies the individual must become self-reliant once more," says Roscher, and he adds: "similar to the way it was at the beginning of every human culture." What Roscher does not see is that in these beginnings individuals were strongly tied to each other by tribal and familial spirit, by habits and customs, by superstitious beliefs and delusions, and that even the rationalism which develops in civilized societies remains inhibited by elements of this kind. Their effect, to be sure, decreases at a certain stage of development, and for this decrease, and also for the maturation of a sober, practical, and calculating rationalism and "individualism," a colonial country offers far more favorable conditions than an old country.

10

SOCIAL VALUES:

ECONOMIC VALUES

Social Entity as the Subject of Social Values

BY VALUES, we understand real or ideal objects as far as they are affirmed, that is, approved, appreciated, loved, admired, revered, or regarded and conceived of with other expressions of love, affection, and pleasure. In these appreciations are contained experiences of the psychic life of individuals. But many values are held in common by many people, for example, objects of nature or of art, in the appreciation of which men of every kind and origin, of any country or zone may have a share, without in other respects having any connections or relations with one another, without even knowing each other or of each other. *Social* values presuppose the existence of a social "entity," that is, a relationship between at least two or possibly several persons, a relationship which exists in the imaginations and thoughts of the participants and to which a common value is attached. As subjects—or shall we say: as members —of such a relationship, they are united in the affirmation of this object, be it that they aspire to or want and desire it, therefore, that they wish to have it in common; or that they have and possess and have in mind to keep it and that they are ready to protect and defend it against the power or hostile intention of others, such as external powers of nature, animals, or humans. Social values are partly economic, partly political, partly spiritual-moral in character. All these are internally related and may blend one into the other. In

---

Translated from *Einfuehrung in die Soziologie*, book 3, chap. 1, pp. 135–49 (§§21, 22, 23, 24, 25).

the present context, we will start with economic values, because they are of high generality.

Common desires, aspirations, and intentions to possess a thing may be based either on hostile or on social feelings—on mutual negation as well as on mutual affirmation. The French King Francis I is supposed to have said wittily: "Mon frère Charles et moi, nous sommes tout d'accord; car nous voulons tous les deux la même chose: Milan." ("My brother Charles V and I, we are in complete agreement; for we both want the same thing: Milan.") Indeed, it happens with regard to the most varied phenomena of social life, that the craving for the same or similar values disunites people and becomes the cause for various, sometimes fatal hostilities: whether from jealousy and envy, one-sided or mutual, in the way of competition or rivalry, where one begrudges the other the possession of an object, hoping to cut him out, to precede and defeat him; or where one wishes to take away, steal, or rob an object of value from another person who has it; or it may be that discord arises in a partition, where the point is for several to divide between them an object, or where pieces of an object are to be divided in equal or varying parts; this occurs easily, because one or several or all want more—or want what they consider to be better—than the others, and are dissatisfied with their share, and angry and annoyed, often convinced, rightly or wrongly, that the distribution had been handled unfairly and that they were wronged. This applies obviously to material or economic values, the enjoyment of which is by its nature individual and exclusive, in other words, a *private* pleasure. To be sure, there exists the custom of common eating and drinking, and this constitutes a popular way of living together, so that the Romans called a feast a *convivium* (a living together). But to like food and drink, to relish and to enjoy it, this everybody can do only for himself. Discord in this case is not likely to arise, among human beings, from a selfish wanting of more, except among children; and yet the "feed trough" has become the image of an object of value around which men throng greedily, quarrel among each other, so that one tries to snatch away from the other his bread— the fodder.

Already among children, one easily observes the contrast between peaceful possession and the enjoyment of common values, and the wish to have it all to oneself or to have more of it, which so often becomes the cause of controversy and noisy contention. The superior power and authority of mother or father or of some other adult person that is respected and feared by the children usually resolves and settles the dispute, even if only for a short while.

Varieties of Property

Wherever permanent living together can be observed, we find the concept of "property" developed as something that in fact or by law "belongs" to one or several persons. By law, that is, according to a social will which everybody normally recognizes as valid, and which has sufficient power to prevail and consequently to settle disputes. Always and everywhere there exists individual or private property as well as collective property in objects which are appreciated as individual or social values. Here arises the big question—an important sociological problem: what comes first, private property or collective property? "First," to be understood, on the one hand, in terms of time, on the other hand, in terms of logic. Something may be later in time but logically, that is, in its imagined essence, earlier. For instance, it is an old argument: what comes earlier, the hen or the egg? Every hen, as one knows, grows from an egg, and yet in its essence, or as it is said, in the idea, the hen is undoubtedly earlier than the egg; even "historically," at any rate, earlier than the egg that is laid by her.

Consequently, regarding property, I consider both cases as logically possible: the one that collective property is considered to be earlier, and private property as arising from it. And the opposite case, that private property is thought of as natural and original, and that all collective property arises from it, in such a way that several persons contribute their share to a common good which they then consider and conceive as their common property. The one as well as the other is logically possible; this means, at the same time, that it is legally possible, if we understand by law that which is established by common will and which is strong enough to assert itself and to be enforced: a configuration of the social norm which occupies a wide area in social life, of living together, by means of the general, or at least sufficiently weighty, authority of the judge as arbiter in disputes: an authority which is manifested most clearly as the uninhibited execution of the will contained in the arbitration.

The different relationship between collective property and private property presupposes a different relationship of persons to one another and to their own collectivity or group. Men can conceive and regard their belonging together, and their union, and thus perhaps their commonwealth or state as something real and necessary, as a body whose members they themselves are. This means that they want it as such and affirm it: this again will be most easily absorbed in their thinking if and insofar as they feel and conceive themselves as essentially belonging together, as is the case when they consider themselves as brothers and call themselves by that name. Indeed, it is relationship through common descent which most easily allows for such feelings and thoughts to grow. In that case, we have common property which, as undivided inheritance, naturally appears as collective property, from which the private property of brothers and sisters derives in the case of subdivision. But also in case of a complete division, something of the idea of collective property remains, as long and insofar as the consciousness and willingness of belonging together and of brotherhood is maintained. Such a feeling, however, may also develop from other causes: not only from *being* together (*Zusammenwesen*), by which I mean the sentiment of belonging together because of blood relationship. It can also develop from living together and acting together, each of which, as a rule, is conditioned through, and evolved from, being together but from which it is more or less detached.

Thus, what I call *Gemeinschaft* among human beings develops also from neighborhood as the general expression of living together, and from friendship, comradeship, fellowship (*Genossenschaft*) as the general expression of acting together. In all relationships of this kind the strict exclusiveness of private property is frequently broken and modified, for instance, through gifts, hospitality, interest-free loans, and many kinds of unilateral or mutual aid: through the gratuitous lending of utensils. In this sense the Greeks had a proverb: common, or communal (*gemeinschaftlich*), is what belongs to friends; and similarly, there is a saying: it's all the same among friends. However, over and above such restricted relationships, these feelings of communality (*Gemeinschaft*) are retained with regard to common goods, even those of an economic nature and pertaining to a great nation, as is expressed in the phrase: "We shall be one people, united as brothers," and in the feeling of the necessity and duty to stand together in defending one's country, the very soil which one inhabits together, even if only a small segment of the total population actually has a share in private property.

I have called the feeling that thus evolves as a willing by the name of essential will (*Wesenwille*), in order to express the thought that it is based on the essence (*Wesen*) of the human mind and of its relation both to fellow men and to things to which it considers itself bound and wishes to be bound. In my system the elements of essential will are: *(1) liking:* this is what we usually call love. But it covers a wider area, being not only the lively and frequently passionate affect which is indicated by the word love but also a quiet feeling of comfort and contentment, which may pass the threshold of consciousness only on the occasion of disturbances and inhibitions, that is, when a loss is threatened or has become a reality. In this subconscious feeling lies the transition to the other element, namely, *(2) habit,* which is often called man's second nature; where we consider as natural that common approving relationship to what we have and enjoy as being part of us, such as the organs or limbs of our own body. It is well known that habit, by means of continual practice, makes all activities easy, strengthens and heightens our abilities; on the other hand, habit lessens suffering, makes what is unpleasant and burdensome bearable, sometimes even dear. Habit strengthens the bonds which tie men to other men, and men to things. This psychic fact, therefore, is of as great and universal importance for human living together as the original element of agreement, that is, liking.

To these is added a third element of essential will: *(3) memory:* that is, the remembrance and the knowledge based on it of the value of the person or thing to which a person feels himself bound. Value here means the good quality, the reliability which is also recognized and appreciated as genuineness and which indicates in perseverance and constancy, in trials, in dangers, and in the midst of evils either that a quality of this kind has been experienced or, at any rate, is confidentially expected. It should be understood that even utility can be an important mark of value in this sense.

Social Foundations of Property

It is psychologically necessary that human beings regard as common property or as social value that which they use and enjoy together, defend together, and have acquired or created together. It is equally necessary, however, that the single individual regards as his special and private property that which he uses and enjoys by himself, holds and defends himself, and, above all, what he alone has acquired and created. These basic elements, or foundations (*Gruende*), of property may harmonize, but they can also collide. It is a general phenomenon that men living together, at least insofar as they acknowledge one another as belonging together, for instance, in the sense indicated above, as brothers, blood relations, members of a tribe or a people, that such men consider the land they inhabit as their common property, because they are determined to defend it. Moreover, the knowledge or at least the opinion is widespread that perhaps not they themselves but their forefathers have acquired and conquered it and taken possession of it; that it is, as it were, "purchased" with their sweat or even with their blood. Moreover, they consider it to be a social value, insofar as they love it as their homeland and as they feel bound to it, perhaps through the burial grounds, in particular those of their parents and ancestors, and therefore feel in duty bound to hold it in high regard.

From these motivations a social consciousness has developed which assumes that the land is, or should be, common property and that this is ideally the right thing. This joint dominion over the land is what is meant when the term original or primitive communism is used, and when the doctrine is asserted that this is generally the original institution, and private property is something late and unnatural, an artificial and enforced limitation of a normal equality, which is expressed by the idea of brotherhood. In actual fact, this original communism is chiefly, but not exclusively, connected with land. In this respect it assumes various shapes and forms, depending on the kind of existing communal (*Gemeinschaft*-like) corporations, which change naturally, especially by becoming larger; as a rule, this happens because more children grow up than are needed as substitutes for dying individuals: a natural increase which essentially is unlimited. The increase of population also has the effect that there is a transition from close and near relationships to distant and far ones, and that even in the most favorable case of a general spatial staying together, the living together somehow gains a wider meaning; it no longer implies living under the same roof or even personal acquaintance as between neighbors; acquaintance, however, normally leads to sexual relationships, to friendship, to social intercourse, and to all kinds of habitual cooperation. The wider spatial dispersion, of course, diminishes the common consciousness, or feeling, that the land is common property, whereas for those living in narrower circles it is retained more easily and more firmly. These kinds of "intercourse" which are mentioned go along well with fully developed private property, the exclusiveness of which may be mitigated by mutual gifts as an expression of congratulations, and in the form of hospitality, patronage, interest-free loans, but also through charity in the ordinary and extraordinary course of events—actions which are possible and real, then, even outside of actual *Gemeinschaft*.

Parallel with this development and caused by it, the feeling of interconnectedness through dwelling together, the general character of which I have designated as neighborhood, happens to appear more and more alongside, and to some degree in place of, the feeling of belonging together through blood relationship (kinship) or through being together (*Zusammenwesen*). In the general historical connection of cultural development, the village community becomes the predominant social corporation in place of the kin group or the clan (gens or sib). Through agriculture the village community has a special connection with the *Mark*, that is, the area which is considered the common property of the fellowship (*Genossenschaft*), even if in addition to cultivated fields this area comprises forest, meadows, water, and wilderness. Indeed, the uncultivated pieces of land are retained in the common consciousness as *social* values, as communal property, even more easily than the tilled soil, as long as the need does not arise, internally or by imposition from the outside, for the land to be parceled out.

For, separate or private property, especially that of a single family, whenever it detaches itself from the clan, particularly if the father of a family appears as the head and master of its belongings, is as natural and as original as the separate existence of every kind of *Gemeinschaft* and its common goods. Thus, within the village community, even where its members appear in other respects as equals and entitled to the same rights, the individual family possesses its own homestead: house, yard, and garden; and the family acquires a special property in the plot of land which in the beginning is only assigned to it for a limited period—until a new and definite division is made somewhat later. This has been the actual development of agri-culture as distinct from agri-nature, as it existed for thousands of years, and is still the case in some areas.

But private property in the tilled land is surrounded by the common property of the village community, and its use is conditioned and dependent on the collective will of the community. This is, purely externally, indicated by the existence of mixed holdings that make strict coordination of all work on the village lands, that is, a compulsory common tillage (*Flurzwang*), a necessity. Plowing and harvesting have to be performed simultaneously by every family. Many and significant remainders of this institution can be observed even today with all peoples who gain their livelihood mainly through the cultivation of grain. This state is usually referred to as communal tillage or champion farming (*Feldgemeinschaft*) and has become the object of endless learned interpretations and disputes.

From Communal Tillage to Private Property

In this connection, communal tillage is particularly important for us, because due to the legislation of the modern state it has been subjected for the last two hundred years to the great process of dissolution. From this the pure, complete, and absolute, that is, unconditional, private landed property has eventually evolved. This development is only one, but one of the most important, of the features which characterize the ascendancy of *Gesellschaft* over *Gemeinschaft* as a sociological phenomenon; in economic history, the same process is designated as the rise and progress of a social order, which, by general consent, is now called capitalistic. For the ownership of capital as far as, according to origin and general character, it is owership of money, as a natural and general private property, stands in contrast to the natural and general communal (*Gemeinschaft*-like) property in land. On the other hand, through the combination of shares as a means to a common end arises from private property the associational (*Gesell-schaft*-like) property.

One may say that common property of the land, even after a derived private property in arable fields and in meadows has developed and become established within the actual community, will assert itself and retain its special significance with regard to forest, water, grazing land, and waste. This is the case independent of possible feudal privileges concerning the same land which may have developed from the overall property of the community or some other more comprehensive cooperative corporation, or fellowship (*Genossenschaft*). Such claims could arise from rights due to conquest or to formal transference, for instance, on religious grounds, to the priesthood. In other words, common tillage and the common property of the land as the economic unit of the village community, sociologically speaking, will remain the manifestation of *Gemeinschaft* as long as it dominates and conditions the economy of each individual peasant or farmer by means of the system of mixed holdings and obligatory common tillage; also the economy of secular and ecclesiastical overlords, who have their share in the land which is communally tilled even though it may not be communally owned. Then there is the common pasture ("common"), which is of great value to the poor copyholders (*Hintersassen*) who, with the increase in population and through settlement in the service of the feudal lords, are left more and more without a share in arable and pasture lands or have to make do with what is insufficient for their household and who, as a result, depend on the sale of their labor. The common pasture has been kept in existence in some areas of Germany as well as in other countries as a remainder of the old system of communal tillage (*Feldgemeinschaft*), and has resisted the division of the common until far into the nineteenth century. This division was the result of legislation in the interest of intensive cultivation, the so-called consolidation of holdings (*Feldbereinigung*), which involved compulsory participation and exchange. It not only abolished the common (*Almende*) as far as it consisted in arable fields and pasture but also destroyed the ancient privilege of free cutting of wood in the forests, and in most cases divided the common pasture. However, in some regions, especially in the mountains, as, for instance, in the Alps, it resisted destruction and has remained a strong and enduring element in the Swiss economy.

The enthusiasm for the unconditional private property, under the common influence of the modern liberal legal doctrine and the system of "political economy," has dominated public opinion as an expression of the common consciousness of the educated upper classes in favor of a capitalistic economy. This enthusiasm no longer has its former force and self-assurance; it has been shaken by the combined effect of the retrograde tendencies, never quite extinct, which are supported mainly by the interests of the old gentry (*Herrenstand*) and the much more powerful effect of the labor movement. A socialistic mode of thinking has gained more and more ground, even if it is shaky ground. Even apart from these two movements—the retrograde romantic movement and the labor movement, which is predominantly based on large industry—a general movement has grown powerfully. For one, it is a movement in favor of the reform of the law concerning landed property and against its mobilization, which is the result of the most unimpeded freedom of disposition in several important countries, including Germany. In particular a new appreciation has grown of municipal and other corporative private property, including state (or national) property, as against the more specifically private property of individuals and families: the thought has arisen that the "tax state" and the "tax community" should be superseded by a state and a municipality working for its own good and thus for the good of all; thus, instead of sustaining public bodies, according to the principle of private law, from the income and the property of individual citizens, so that, although these contributions are compulsory, they remain dependent on the solvent rich—rather, the public corporations should be established alongside and above the power of the wealthy private owners as independent powers representing the multitude of more or less impecunious citizens—in other words, as the power of labor against the power of capital.

Private property, on the one hand, has a purely individual meaning, as there exists a property of objects which a person has to have for his own use only, such as his comb and his toothbrush, or his food and drink. Socioeconomic theory is not concerned with this kind of property. However, the other kind of private property is of immeasurable social significance. It is the power inherent in a man or a number of associated persons enabling them to make other people give up what they have and to engage in many kinds of voluntary actions. This *Gesellschaft*-like private property is crystallized as the possession of money. Money is essentially an idea, the idea of the *Gesellschaft*-like commodity, which corresponds to all real commodities because each is soluble into a quantity of it, and which consequently can be divided into equal quantities. Its essence does not change by its being represented by some definite and concrete commodity, whether its substance is valued for its inherent quality or whether this substance, in itself unessential and worthless, has nevertheless obtained by means of a form of social will—convention or law—the quality of validity. This is possible only if the owner feels sure, more or less permanently, of this validity, that is, of a sufficiently definite value for which the money could at any time, or at least during an unlimited time, be exchanged for a variety of other goods. In this sense, money is nothing but purchasing power, therefore essentially the potential for the acquisition of goods. Potentiality signifies a certain degree of probability, and even the above-mentioned ideally complete subjective certainty is in reality—objectively considered—at best a high degree of probability. But the claim or the demand to obtain a commodity, therefore also any kinds of goods, including the gen-

eralized commodity, money, has possibly an equally or similarly
high degree of probability in a *Gesellschaft*-like system, especially
one that is protected by the laws of the state. The most definite kind
of such a claim is the one that is stated in terms of a certain sum of
money. The more the objective probability of fulfillment of such
a claim approaches the objective probability of the validity of a
certain sum of money, the more, then, a subjective certainty derives from the objective probability, the more will the value of a
claim equal the value of the sum of money required for it. The
concept of private property of money, therefore, extends through
the property of claims to the concept of wealth.

In a *Gesellschaft*-like sense, there exists common property in
goods of any kind, thus also in sums of money and in claims: in
other words, common or *Gesellschaft*-like wealth. The special property of the individual does not arise here from common property;
rather common property is formed out of the contributions or in-
vestments of several individuals. In the same way that his wealth
signifies nothing else for a person than a means for obtaining goods
or pleasures or the services of others, thus the investment, the share,
is a means to a comparable end which the investor expects and
hopes to attain more easily through a combination of means.

Among these ends, one is of special significance: it does not
aim directly at obtaining goods in order to possess, keep, and enjoy
them, but in order to dispose of them again, and this with as much
profit as possible. To this end, money is an especially suitable, if
not the only, means to obtain, by its use, a larger amount of it,
which is profit. Applied in this way, a sum of money is called capital. Insofar as money is the more capable of such achievements
the more it is amassed, capital fulfills its end as associated capital,
the capital of an association (*Gesellschaft*). For us it is of interest
only in that it represents an important form of private property: the
property of an association or a corporation in which several private
owners have shares, so that the property of the individual is perpet-
uated in the *Gesellschaft*-like property, even though it amounts to
no more than a mere claim. At least there is a claim to a share in
profits whenever the association (*Gesellschaft*) acknowledges,
through its proper representatives, the existence of such a profit

which can be divided and distributed. The difference and contrast between *Gemeinschaft* and *Gesellschaft* are reflected here in the different kind of social value, as a value of economic commodities, and the different kind of relationship toward individual value and property.

It must suffice to draw attention here to the worldwide significance of this *Gesellschaft*-like property as the power of capitalism. Capitalism, whose elementary manifestations are to be seen in trade and in the lending of money, rises to perfection as the capitalistic production of commodities, from which follows the capitalistic domination of the means of communication and also of intellectual life inasfar as the latter is based on both communication and production. The essence of capitalistic production consists in the fact that, just as other commodities, labor, too, as the ability to produce commodities, can be bought. Through the combination of its services and of the material means of production through which it works, new commodities are produced by means of individual or societal (associational) capital, the sale of which, as a rule, results in a profit of greater or smaller extent; the aim always being profit as large and at the same time as safe as possible.[1]

---

[1]   Toennies means to say that profit from invested capital is the basic principle of capitalism.—Eds.

11

SOCIAL VALUES:

ETHICAL SOCIAL VALUES

Institutions, Persons, and Things

I DISTINGUISH as such, (1) institutions, (2) persons, (3) things, (4) memories, (5) signs.

Institutions.—The political values (for example, fatherland, state, constitution) are at the same time ethical values insofar as they are acknowledged and approved by a moral consciousness; this means, not only from habit, or conventionally, or merely from moods, or for their usefulness and comfort, but from an attitude of respect and reverence. A sentiment of this kind, as a rule, preferably is bestowed upon old age, including that of institutions. It may also be based on a feeling for, or in recognition of, its expediency, on trust and hope, and it is, like ethical sentiments in general, related to aesthetic feelings, notwithstanding many differences between the two. Toward no other institutions is this sentiment so strong as it is toward religious institutions, if we refer to those who relate to these institutions as believers. Reverence in this case expresses itself through the predicate of holiness, meaning venerability and inviolability—predicates attributed to religion itself, and above all to the Church as a union which is even declared to be supernatural; a social entity, then, of the highest sublimity. However, the actual sanctified objects are not so much invisible entities but invisible persons imagined as visible, supermen or gods, objects of all kinds of cults, according to their nature exaggerated creations of a veneration otherwise offered to human beings that are

Translated from *Einfuehrung in die Soziologie*, book 3, chap. 3, pp. 169–86 (§§30, 31, 32, 33).

admired and feared: thus to the aged, to ancestors, to the dead in general, to kings and princes. At this point the veneration of humans changes into the veneration of gods or at least demigods. All institutions, thus also the state, the community, are human institutions, but acquire easily, especially when sanctified by age, the quality of divinity.

Living persons.—Living persons can also be appreciated as economic values, can even be objects of property, as slaves or serfs, who because of their usefulness, but possibly also for their own sakes, are appreciated, loved, and even pampered. This is most likely the case if sexual relationships are involved. Living persons are also regarded as political values in popular consciousness and in the considerations of statesmen, especially because of their significance for military purposes, for the defense of the country, and even for the conquest of foreign countries. It is in close connection with this that persons because of their high rank, hereditary or acquired, are regarded as social values, particulary when they are called upon to exercise the functions of a master and ruler, whether directly by virtue of the glamour in which they appear or because they have attracted admiration, gratitude, and awe through their achievements, apparent or real. This has happened at all times, in the first place to victorious military heroes, especially when they appear as saviors from great dangers and as liberators from serious troubles, such as oppressive foreign rule or other tyrannies. A particularly high esteem is bestowed upon the military profession and generally on men bearing arms, not only by women; in this respect, women are representatives of the common people. Admiration of heroism may be extended to persons who have nothing heroic about them: colorful uniforms and shining armor excite the senses and engage the imagination, especially of women and children.

Other persons may appear equally venerable, namely, those who have made themselves known as benefactors or saviors in wider or smaller circles; to these belong, the more superstition attaches to them, sorcerers and priests and eremites who are considered holy and men and women who are thought of as sages, radiating beneficial effects or feared because of harmful ones, such as witches and sorcerers. But political leaders, statesmen, or leaders of parties, too, can arouse praise, enthusiasm, and love, and are paid homage to and esteemed as if they were gifts sent from heaven. Gradually, moreover, in periods of advanced urban civilization, while the circle of those who appreciate and honor in the old manner becomes smaller, such admiration is bestowed, although to a lesser degree, on other achievements which are considered to be in some way useful or enjoyable or both, and on persons to whom they are attributed: achievements in science and art, in particular those that appeal to the masses and are accessible to popular understanding, like dramatic art when it moves people to tears or produces hilarious laughter. All in all, the more life becomes public, the more the attention of those who read or attend at spectator arts is drawn to strange and extraordinary objects and persons, partly quite naturally, partly by various kinds of artifices, the sooner will objects of admiration become objects of a cult of some sort, even if often only for a short while, as we contemporaries have experienced constantly in the rush and fickleness of present-day metropolitan life. Even as early as in the *turbida Roma* of the emperors, one man was raised to the throne of admiration today, and another tomorrow, and to many a man hosanna was shouted who was, the week after, considered a candidate for crucifixion. Thus we observe today that some champion, like a skilled swimmer, especially a lady swimmer, or a victorious boxer or wrestler, would be praised and feted more than, say, a meritorious poet, musician, or artist, who may be waiting in vain for applause. Even today, as happened more easily in times past under simpler conditions, men may be held in esteem for their virtues by small circles, perhaps as teachers or masters in their art or as plain citizens, even if nothing but the beneficial effect of their life and conduct is observed, and they are contrasted with the many others who have the opposite effect. Sentiments and thoughts of this kind have sometimes bestowed upon such men and women a halo which in churches has given them the quality of saints, by means of which they could attain a sublimity superior even to that of high secular rank and its glamour.

Deceased persons.—All effects of this kind by which living persons are transformed into social values are concentrated to a higher degree upon distinguished persons who are no longer alive. In a way, *worship of the dead* has always been practiced, at least by a small group of relatives and friends, if only as the last respect paid to the deceased, through care for and decoration of his grave, even if otherwise he was a most obscure person. The intensity and duration of a cult of this kind are largely dependent on the prosperity of the bereft; the rich may set a magnificent memorial to a stillborn child, and in other ways, too, burial places are often used as conspicuous demonstrations of an elevated status as much as for their aesthetic effect. Among such admirers—apparent or real —of their dead, most naturally princes and kings and the like have always been noticeable: the tomb of an otherwise insignificant prince of Caria has given his name to what was after him called a mausoleum. Herbert Spencer has suggested that temples evolved from burial places; this is quite probable, transitions being manifold, even if almost imperceptible, from the gifts accompanying the corpses to the contributions and sacrifices dedicated to them. Of these, wreaths and flowers are the remainders in our time: from sacrifices offered to the dead to sacrifices offered to the gods. Ancestor worship has been retained as a noble custom probably by the largest part of the human race. It makes its appearance in all regions where the Church cultivates the traditional superstition of the cult of souls and tolerates it as part of its ideology. It is most probable that these cults represent the original form of a religious mode of thinking which has receded in the high religions of the Orient and Occident increasingly behind the more glamorous cults of deities of a more universal validity and their prophets, or even of an only or trinitarian God, or his Son, or the Holy Ghost.

Things.—Thus objects of many kinds may be spiritual (*ideell*) and ethical values for small or large social entities. For holy pictures and reliques are valued and honored not because of their exchange or money value, which, to be sure, may play its part, but like other, even possibly insignificant, objects, for their own sake or for the sake of the associations with which they are connected in the minds of those who honor them. Their use value is not essential or may be nonexistent; their value is of an affective nature, perhaps for a few, perhaps for many. The same holds true for all objects of secular or religious adoration, such as temples, church buildings, chapels, and memorials of every kind; it holds for holy objects of religions, equally for unholy ones, if they once belonged to men of worldly fame: they may be valued as private property or, if they are represented in museums—as saints are in churches—as social values. In the imagination of the faithful, pictures always symbolize relics of the person, the god or the hero whom they represent. "The identity of the god and his idol remains a widespread assumption far beyond the stage of primitive religion." Even "apart from similarity, participation or physical contact are sufficient for creating such a causal relationship." (Spencer) Thus rises "the practice of regarding nails, hair curls, clothes, arms, or implements of a person as if it were a complete substitute for this person"; one believes one can gain power over him by means of such objects, one loves and admires them for this reason, and they become ideal social values.

In matters like these, memory is the initial factor, even for someone who has not known the long deceased or mythical person, that inclines the soul to devotion. In the same way, memories become social values of a spiritual (*ideell*) or ethical nature, even if a factual substance is lacking.

Memories

Common memories.—As memories unite a pair of friends or a married couple, a family small or large, and many are cultivated lovingly, so there are no *Gemeinschaft*-like collectives or corporations that do not revere or even keep sacred some common memories; these are memories of common actions and suffering and of persons who had been prominent in their circle. Here, too, fighters and saviors are in the front row, but others may also be praised as popular benefactors; to them a memorial is set in some form, they are remembered in speech and song, and celebrations are held in their memory. A feast is especially destined to keep alive or reawaken memories: in the family, birthdays, weddings, and other anniversaries are celebrated; rarer occasions are silver and golden weddings or a birthday if it signifies a considerable num-

ber of years. Such days have the effect that even more distant relatives, friends, and acquaintances, not to mention strangers, take
part in the festive day of remembrance and feel impelled to demonstrate this on account of their sentiments but occasionally also
because they suppose that this may be useful to them. In this way,
a whole country may express its sentiments toward eminent men
and women who enjoy its admiration and upon whom it feels
obliged to bestow its gratitude. In particular a people who, as a
nation, has a common memory can give expression to sentiments
of admiration and gratitude by means of monuments or works of
art or through festivals; an example is the unveiling of a monu-
ment on the occasion of a centenary or the day of remembrance
of a birth or death that occurred several centuries ago. Mnemosyne
was revered in Greece as the mother of the muses and, as one of the
muses, Klio, the muse of history. In fact, it is the principal function of history and that of the muses in general to cultivate and
promote the common memories of a people. This is most noticeable for wider circles where a people really live together, in the
sense of a knowledge of its past, a knowledge dependent, like all
knowledge, on the wish to know, on a lively interest which therefore presupposes a certain degree of education and can thus be
promoted through instruction. Instruction is ususally carried on
under religious or political sponsorship; as a result, it may be directed either to cultivate mainly the memory of religious values
and their carriers—founders of religions, church dignitaries,
priests—or toward the memory of princes or, in a long-established
republic, of persons who are of historical importance in the history
of that republic. In this sense, the arts, especially poetry, which in
themselves are social values of great significance, are likewise of
value for the purpose of enhancing and glorifying common memories. Poetry belongs to a festive celebration, together with music
in which its charms are heightened, like a beautiful garment belongs to a beautiful figure.

Gesellschaft-like entities, too, gladly take advantage of the op-
portunity to celebrate jubilees and to imitate the outward manifestations of *Gemeinschaft*-like life: partly for reasons of senti-
mentality regarding the persons involved, partly because it is good

for business and serves as publicity. In this way, all *Gemeinschaft*-like life, living together, celebrating together, is constantly in danger of conventionalization; more often than not, it rigidifies and ends up a mere shadow of itself.

Fame

A social value, which as a quality, an ornament, as it were, is ascribed to things or persons, natural things as well as works of art, is fame. One must understand fame as an expression of social will, because its foundation is acknowledgment, gratitude, the admiration of many, in a higher sense of an entire people, in the rarest and highest instance of all humanity. Fame exists often to a far lesser degree and extent than is imagined, particularly by those who believe they possess it. Even where it is genuine and real, it attaches only to the name, whereas the real merits which it is meant to designate may be known to only a few and appreciated by even fewer. Also, fame is often of a fleeting nature, swiftly blown away, like the rumor which carries it. Fame is meant to signify ethical value, in contrast to notoriety. Yet, both have to do with being much talked about, and with the imagination of something interesting and memorable that attaches to the names and their bearers. Thus, the value of fame is easily overestimated; not only because its genuineness, as that of other highly esteemed objects, is more frequently assumed than might correspond to the truth; even more so because it usually is of shorter duration than one may think. That is why the fame of the dead has always been considered to be greater than that of the living, and it is not infrequently bestowed on people who were little known and little talked about during their lifetime. Thus, posthumous fame is considered to be the true fame: the memory and gratitude of later generations for achievements which have proved their value, increased their significance, and are diffused far and wide.

If Schiller, a poet-historian, makes a Homeric hero say, "Of all life's goods, fame is the greatest," he was thinking, in the first place, of martial fame, of the heroism which has always been the prime object of popular admiration. But much heroism of this kind, thus also the fame which is attached to it, fades in the course of centuries, like the splendor and glitter of precious things which once had made the deepest impression on their contemporaries. More lasting is the fame which is a reward for lasting achievements, especially if their memory is celebrated in song, or if still in our day and in the days to come the works of great poets and thinkers continue to delight and warm their readers' hearts, as they have made happy their long-lost contemporaries thousands of years ago.

Shortlived celebrity sounds off, but, apart from varying duration, shows varying extent and magnitude, sometimes conceived of as heights—as pointed out in Homer's "Tu gar kleos uranon hikei" ("His renown rises to the heights of heaven"). In truth, many men consider it a privilege merely to have their name mentioned, better still, to have it mentioned often, most of all, to have it passed on to posterity. Herostratos the Ephesian, obsessed by this ambition, set fire to the temple of Artemis, and although at the time the cities of Ionia took it upon themselves never to mention his name, yet he was "successful." Many an ambition is no more noble than that.

Signs and Symbols

Signs.—As a fifth and a very significant type of social value I regard social signs. Social signs are distinguished from individual ones: sense perceptions and memories are effective as signs with reference to objects or movements, thus also with reference to human actions, if they induce the preceiving or remembering individual—animal or human—to a certain kind of willing or feeling, thinking or acting. The most important effect of this kind is the inference, for which in many cases signs become the cause without their perception attaining the level of consciousness. A sign is what is effective as a sign. One concludes from signs that something exists, or used to exist, or is going to exist. On the one hand, signs are natural, that is, those that were not, and probably could not be, willed to be signs, such as a meteroic appearance that rouses pleasant or somber expectations; on the other hand, signs are willed, that is, they are made, given, set, with the intention that they have the effect of signs, meaning that they are interpreted and understood as such; often they also mean that something ought to be done. Such signs may be natural signs made for some useful purpose, like the affectation of a gesture, or they are invented for their purpose and are actually artificial signs. The former, like the latter, are individual signs as long as by their very nature they have the effect of signs and are understood as such. They do not become social signs because several individuals apply them, not even when these individuals use them simultaneously for a definite purpose, for example, in order to make some impression upon animals or humans. A natural or willed, especially an artificial, sign becomes a social sign only by serving several individuals, on the basis of a quality which is commonly known and serviceable to these several individuals, in such a way that it has the same effect on all participants, that it is understood and consequently correctly interpreted by all.

Only a social will creates social signs. Consequently, the most rational and therefore the most clear and distinct kind of social willing is the decision made by several persons conjointly that a thing or action ought to be a sign for them, the decision makers; this is the simplest origin of a social sign. Not essentially different from this is the agreement, except that, like the decision by a small number, it may be between only two persons. Agreed-upon signs have always played an important and manifold part in social life. They are most significant if the agreed-upon signs are secret signs, that is, if it is of their essence to be known exclusively to those who have agreed upon them. In this way love signs, for instance, if a flower or color of a certain kind was agreed upon, may serve as a sign to meet at a certain time or place. But intimate signs, even if they are not agreed or decided upon, may be accepted as valid in some circle of persons if their meaning is shared by giver and receiver.

Language.—This is the most significant system of such signs imparted through audible sounds, possibly designed only for one-sided understanding like commands which are also understood by some animals; as a rule, however, they serve for mutual under-